MEDITATION DYNA

New Edition

Learn How to Meditate
For Self-Realization, Serenity, Intuitive Guidance,
Success, and Mystical Illumination

DR. PAUL LEON MASTERS, FOUNDER
International Metaphysical Ministry
University of Metaphysics
University of Sedona

Meditation Dynamics
New Edition

University of Sedona Publishing
1785 W. State Route 89A, Suite 3G
Sedona, Arizona 86336
www.universityofsedona.com

All rights reserved.
Copyright © 2022 International Metaphysical Ministry.
Protected under International and U.S. Federal
Copyright Laws and Treaties. Any unauthorized reprint or
use of this material is prohibited. No part may be reproduced
or transmitted in any form or by any means, electronic or mechanical,
including photocopying, digitizing, recording,
or by any information storage and retrieval system
without express written permission by the
Board of Directors of the
International Metaphysical Ministry.

Library of Congress Control Number: 2022913819
Masters, Paul Leon.
Meditation Dynamics
/ Paul Leon Masters. – New Edition
ISBN 978-0-9964596-6-2
1. Meditation.   2. Mind and Body.   3. Metaphysics.

Disclaimer

The content of this book is not intended to replace any form of professionally licensed care, be it medical, psychological, or any other licensed health modality. The views and ideas expressed, whether in totality or as an adjunct to one's spiritual or religious beliefs, are for use in one's Spiritual life. Nothing in the content of this book should be considered as infallible, as life is an ongoing process of awakening to truths and practices known only to God.

PRINTED IN THE UNITED STATES OF AMERICA

Also by Dr. Paul Leon Masters

Mystical Insights

Spiritual Mind Power Affirmations

TABLE OF CONTENTS

Foreword vii
Preface ix
Introduction 1

MYSTICAL MEDITATION

Practicing Mystical Meditation 5
A Basic Meditation Method 8
Meditation Variations 13
Candle Concentration Techniques 15
Instantaneous Meditation 21
Guided Meditation 22

AFFIRMATIVE MEDITATION

Practicing Affirmative Meditation 27
Affirming Health of the Body 31
Affirming Health of the Mind 34
Affirming Financial Health and Prosperity 37
Affirming Positive Changes in Your Life 40
Sleep Programming 44

SUGGESTIVE SELF-HYPNOSIS

Practicing Suggestive Self-Hypnosis 49
Hypnotic Pendulum Technique 52
Total Body Relaxation Technique 55
Deep Sleep Candle Technique 60
Waking (Eyes Open) Self-Hypnosis 62

SELF-HYPNOTIC MEDITATION

Practicing Self-Hypnotic Meditation 67
Mystical Self-Hypnosis 68
Deep Sleep Candle Technique II 72

TESTING SELF-HYPNOSIS

Putting Self-Hypnosis to the Test 77
Eyelid Closure Test 78
Rigid Arm Test 80
Handclasp Test 82
Hand Levitation Test 84

MORE TESTS AND TOOLS

Chevreul Pendulum Test 89
Ideomotor Finger Test 93
Testing a Suggestion During Hypnosis 95
Visualization 97
Inner Vision Expansion 101

A METAPHYSICAL WAY OF LIFE

Living Metaphysically 105
Controlling Your Thoughts 106
Controlling Your Words 109
Controlling Cycles in Your Life 112
Attuning Through Your Daily Activities 118
Daily Format for Living Metaphysically 121

About the Author 123
Advanced Metaphysical Studies 125
More Spiritual Resources 127

FOREWORD

I had no idea when I first met Dr. Paul Leon Masters in 1994—which prompted me to register with the University of Metaphysics, obtain my first degree in 1996, and have the honor of serving as an Associate Minister at University Church in Las Vegas—that it would lead to the lifetime of study, service, and satisfaction that it has. During that time, I would have welcomed a book such as this. Fortunately, the ideas, concepts, and encouragement for the daily process of meditation for contacting the Presence of God were already being taught by Dr. Masters.

Although I have been practicing meditation on a regular basis for many years, I have still found in this book words of wisdom and new ways of approaching meditation to help provide balance in my life. This is a book you will want to read more than once—possibly highlighting passages, as I have, to look back on from time to time.

Dr. Masters once told me, "The word 'meditate' simply means to ponder. You give yourself to the practice of meditation in order to receive that which is for your growth and understanding, and also to become a channel of blessings to others in your life."

You go into meditation to commune with the God-Power within you, and to enjoy the inner renewal of mind and body that kind of communion can bring, and to get ideas and guidance from that indwelling intelligence to apply to your daily life.

This book will not only show you why should meditate, but how.

Whether you have been meditating for some time or are new to the process, this book will bring you closer to contacting the Presence of God within you. I believe it will become the standard by which other books on the subject will be judged. I think you will both enjoy and benefit from reading it.

~ Richard P. (Dick) Caldwell D.Min., Vice President
International Metaphysical Ministry

PREFACE

Dr. Paul Leon Masters has been considered by many to be foremost in guiding people into and through meditation. Before his passing in 2016, Dr. Masters spent more than five decades researching meditation and the higher states of consciousness that can be experienced through that practice. In *Meditation Dynamics* you will find the majority of the meditational tools, techniques, and methods that Dr. Masters developed or refined during that time.

What's different about this new edition of *Meditation Dynamics* is that it has been revised and reorganized to present Dr. Masters' teachings in an order that is easier to follow, and it includes additional explanatory material based on Dr. Masters' courses and lectures.

Now, each chapter and section lays a foundation for the next, and a clearer distinction is made between Mystical Meditation, Affirmative Meditation, and Suggestive Self-Hypnosis. Plus, for even greater clarity and understanding, additional instructions and details have been added to some of the techniques and practices that Dr. Masters shares.

It is our hope that this new edition of *Meditation Dynamics* presents Dr. Masters' teachings in a way that best reflects his exceptional work in this field.

~ Rev. Steven Lane Taylor, Editor
University of Sedona Publishing

MEDITATION DYNAMICS

New Edition

DR. PAUL LEON MASTERS

University of Sedona Publishing
Sedona, Arizona

INTRODUCTION

Meditation is the path to peace. It is the way to wisdom. It is the key to a life of lasting happiness and fulfillment, and the secret for experiencing greater success, love, and creativity in your life. Almost everything that is important to you in life—from your physical health to your mental and emotional health to your financial health—is improved through a daily practice of meditation.

There are basically two types of meditation: Mystical Meditation and Affirmative Meditation. Mystical Meditation (also called Contact Meditation) is for the sole purpose of achieving a higher state of consciousness, one in which you are in contact with Universal Consciousness, or the Mind of God, that dwells in the deepest, innermost center of your mind. Affirmative Meditation (also called Self-Programming or Control Meditation) is primarily for the purpose of programming your mind with thoughts that can help you improve your outer life.

Both types of meditation are extremely valuable, because together they can help you reach your full potential as a person who is both inwardly knowing and aware, and at the same time outwardly successful and positive. For that reason, *Meditation Dynamics* offers "how-to" instructions in the practices of both Mystical Meditation and Affirmative Meditation.

Closely related to Affirmative Meditation is Suggestive Self-Hypnosis. You will find that this book offers detailed practices in that effective method of self-programming, as well.

There are many books on meditation in the world, and most are filled with good information about the philosophy and psychology of meditation. However, few—if any—include information about actual meditation methods and self-programming practices to the degree and with the amount of detail you will find in these pages.

MYSTICAL MEDITATION

PRACTICING MYSTICAL MEDITATION

As mentioned in the Introduction, Mystical Meditation is for the sole purpose of achieving a higher state of consciousness, one in which you are in contact with Universal Consciousness, or the Mind of God, that dwells in the deepest, innermost center of your mind.

When practiced daily, mystical union or oneness with the indwelling Presence of God can not only be established, but to some degree it can also be maintained. The more the surface level of your mind remains open and receptive to the influence of Universal Intelligence or God-Mind, the more benefits you will experience.

BENEFITS OF MEDITATION

The benefits of establishing and maintaining closer contact with the Consciousness of God within you include, but are not limited to:

- A calmer, more peaceful state of mind as you go through your day

- A mind that is intuitively guided and more clearly sees what decisions to make

- Increased confidence that comes from knowing you are divinely supported

- More creative ideas you can use to improve your occupation, career, and income

- Increased energy as you tap into the energy of the Universe within you

- Being more loving and attracting love, or keeping the love attraction you already have

- Finding that you are maintaining good health, or that you can find or assist in the physical and/or emotional healing you need

- Finding that you are looking more attractive as the inner beauty of God's Light shines through you

- A better awareness of what your soul's purpose is for this lifetime, and how to live that purpose

In short, by establishing and maintaining a closer connection to the indwelling Presence of God through a daily practice of meditation, you bring forth into your life all of God's attributes—attributes of love, peace, power, creativity, abundance, health, wisdom, and more.

MEDITATION PREPARATION

Before you begin a meditation practice at home, it is important for you to create a proper atmosphere for it. Here are some suggestions:

- Pick a place in your home where there is the least likelihood of your being disturbed.

- The temperature in the room or place where you meditate should be somewhere between 72 and 78 degrees F. If it is too cold, it might draw too much of your attention. If it is too warm, you might fall asleep.

- If it is not too distracting, soft and ethereal music playing in the background may be beneficial.

- Incense may also be helpful, especially the scents of rose, jasmine, or sandalwood.

- Wear loose, comfortable clothing—nothing binding. If you can wear the same thing every time you meditate, that's even better.

- You may practice meditation either sitting up or lying down. Since it is too easy to fall asleep when lying down, beginners should practice in a sitting position for about a week, and then experiment to see which is better—sitting or reclining.

- If you practice sitting in a chair, which is recommended, position your body as follows:

- o Both feet flat on the floor
- o Hands resting palms up on your lap
- o Body erect, but comfortable

- If you practice in a reclining position, position your body as follows:

  - o Have your ankles crossed.
  - o Fold your hands and place them over the central, upper part of your body.
  - o If possible, place your head to the north and your feet to the south.

- Don't meditate when you are hungry, and avoid meditation immediately after a meal, when your body is digesting.

- Before you begin your meditation, you might want to start by imagining that your body is surrounded and protected by a pure, white, spiritual light, and that nothing harmful can penetrate this light.

- Although you might start with only a 5-minute meditation practice, building up to at least a 20-minute practice is best—once every morning, and again in the evening, if possible.

- At first, you may want to use a timer to gauge the length of your meditation, but eventually your own "internal time-clock" should take over.

MOST IMPORTANTLY:

- **Meditate daily! Meditate in the same place each day, and at the same time or times. This daily repetition of time and place and atmosphere will trigger your mind to relax into a meditative state more quickly.**

A BASIC MEDITATION METHOD

Whether you are practicing Mystical Meditation or Affirmative Meditation, the goal is always to quiet the surface level of your personal mind with its many back-to-back thoughts. In the case of Mystical Meditation, this gives any expression of consciousness at the deeper levels of your mind a chance to surface and become more apparent to you.

QUIETING THE MIND

Since it is difficult—if not impossible—to quiet your mind by simply deciding to "stop thinking," the next best thing you can do is to concentrate on only one solitary thing. Your focus of attention may be:

- **YOUR BREATHING**. A common meditation technique is to concentrate on the sensation of your chest rising and falling as you inhale and exhale. You might begin by silently counting to 5 as you slowly inhale, and again as you slowly exhale. Eventually, however, the goal is just to breathe naturally without trying to control it.

- **A MANTRA**. A mantra is a word, sound, or short phrase you silently repeat to yourself over and over in your mind. The most common mantra is the sound of "Om" or "Aum" (pronounced ahh-ooo-mmm). Other words or phrases will also work, but it is best if you choose a word or phrase that doesn't trigger distracting thoughts.

- **A COMBINATION** of the above. Combining a mantra with a focus on your breathing also works well. For instance, after slowly inhaling you might choose to mentally "hear" the sound of "Om" as you slowly release your breath.

The examples above are to be practiced with your physical eyes closed, but directed toward the interior center of your forehead, which is the location of your inner eye or mind's eye, also called the "Third Eye."

As other thoughts arise and interfere with your focus—as they invariably will—you observe those thoughts, but you don't let yourself get caught up in them. Instead, you simply allow those thoughts to pass by—like watching clouds floating across the sky—and you gently return your attention to what you are focusing on.

If you suddenly discover that your mind has wandered far from your focus and you have gotten lost in a train of thought, don't judge yourself for that. It happens to the most accomplished meditators! Once again, simply release those thoughts and go back to concentrating on the focus of your attention.

By quieting your mind with a single focus of attention instead of entertaining one thought after another, your mind is less crowded and less noisy. This creates an atmosphere that is more conducive for direct contact to occur between your surface level of consciousness and, ultimately, the deeper, underlying Consciousness of God.

CONTACT EXPERIENCES

In a deep meditative state, when a state of higher consciousness has been reached, you might have what could be called a "contact experience." With your inner vision you might see any of the following in your Third Eye area, usually accompanied by a feeling of elevation or inspiration:

- **COLORS** – Often appearing in your mind as mist-like clouds. *[NATURAL STATE ✓]*

- **A VORTEX** – A funnel effect, as color seems to flow out from your inner eye and narrow down to a point in the distance. *[DMT]*

- **FLOWERS** – Such as roses, lilies, a lotus blossom, or other flowers. These are the psyche's symbols of higher consciousness.

- **RELIGIOUS SYMBOLS** – They may be orthodox in nature, such as the Holy Cross or the Star of David. Or, they may be more esoteric, such as an urn of fire, a flaming torch, a diamond, or some other jewel.

- **RELIGIOUS FIGURES** – These people, who emanate a definite religious aura in either dress or radiance, are usually visual personifications of a part of your own higher consciousness. *[natural]*

- **BIRDS** – Eagles and doves are the most frequently perceived. Like religious figures, they are usually visual personifications of a part of your own higher consciousness. *[DMT]*

- **SCENES** – Quite common are streets of gold or ornate golden gates. Other scenes also common to higher consciousness are mountains, trees, temples, churches, shrines, stained glass windows, or scenes that can only be from other dimensions.

- **FIRE** – It may be perceived in the head area or inside the upper half of your body. Or, your whole body may be perceived as a flame of fire. After perception, you are usually left feeling psychically or spiritually cleansed. *[DMT]*

- **GEOMETRIC PATTERNS** – These sacred geometrical designs, such as the one pictured on the cover of this book, can arise when you are in a state of psychic wholeness. *[natural]*

- **ASTRAL LIGHT** – This inner light is perceived as an observer. You see it, but you are not one with it. You maintain a separate sense of personal selfhood.

Instead of having a visual contact experience, you might have an audible one. Audible perceptions include:

- **A BEE-LIKE SOUND** – A humming or buzzing type of sound from within the head. This is a phenomenon of consciousness, but not necessarily of higher consciousness.

- **A POUNDING SOUND** – Usually starts softly and then increases in intensity. Similar to bee-like sounds, this is a phenomenon of consciousness, but not necessarily of higher consciousness.

- **THE SOUND OF OM** – Sounds like either "Om" or "Aum," as if it is being breathed within your head. This is definitely a contact with Universal Being.

- **THE MUSIC OF THE SPHERES** – A very melodious, ethereal, or out-of-this-world type of music, sometimes heard with a chorus of voices. In this higher state of consciousness you are in contact with Universal rhythm or motion.

A contact experience can also be felt physically. You might have a sense of:

- **WARMTH** – Your body feels as if it is glowing with a warm and inspiring sense of peace.

- **A FLOW** – You feel pleasant waves of energy flowing up or down your body.

- **SUSPENSION** – Your body feels suspended, as if it is in space, and you feel blissful and joyous.

Finally, you may have the ultimate contact experience:

- **ONENESS WITH GOD** — This sense of Oneness with All is beyond intellectual realization, and it is what all mystics strive for. Your experience may include:

    o Seeing a pure, white Inner Light—the very Light of God—and becoming one with that Light and losing all sense of a personal selfhood.

    o Feeling a peaceful emotional release.

    o Sensing that the whole Universe has stopped for One Eternal Moment, and you are experiencing that One Eternal Moment.

    o Feeling like you are one with the Universe and flowing with the Total Beingness of Life.

Whatever kind of contact experience you have during your meditation—visual, audible, or physical—stay with it for as long as possible, or for as long as you feel comfortable doing so.

If you don't have any kind of contact experience—and most often you will not—you will still find that because of your daily meditation practice your personal consciousness will be more open and receptive to the influence and intuitive guidance of Universal Consciousness and Ultimate Intelligence throughout the day. As stated before, the benefits of a daily practice of meditation are many, improving every single aspect of your life.

MEDITATION VARIATIONS

If you are having trouble quieting your mind by simply focusing on your breathing or silently repeating a mantra, here are three variations to help you still your thoughts and shift your consciousness from a sense of outer awareness to a heightened sense of inner awareness.

OUTER SENSE CLOSURE TECHNIQUE

For the first five minutes of your meditation, do the following:

1. Using both hands, place your index fingers on your temples.
2. Place your middle fingers lightly on your eyelids.
3. Place your ring fingers gently on either side of your nasal passages.
4. Place your thumbs comfortably resting in your ears.
5. Place your little fingers gently in the edges of your mouth.

After 5 minutes relax your hands and arms and continue your meditation practice as usual.

AUM BREATHING TECHNIQUE

The sacred sound of "Aum" represents the vibration through which the universe—and everything in it—was brought into manifestation.

As previously mentioned, you can quiet your mind by repeating the sound of "Aum" silently to yourself as a mantra. But you can also achieve good results if you begin your meditation by first chanting "Aum" out loud for a few minutes.

For maximum results, you may want to practice the following method, known only to a few advanced mystics:

1. Breath in with your mouth slightly open, letting the "A" (as in "ahh") be formed by the sound of your inhaling breath.

2. With your mouth still slightly open, the first half of your exhalation forms the "U" sound (as in "ooo").

3. Then, for the second half of your exhalation, with your mouth closed let the breath that is passing through your nostrils form the "M" sound (as in "mmm").

Do this about seven times consecutively, and then continue your meditation practice as usual. The vibration achieved by breathing "Aum" in this manner will help stimulate a state of higher consciousness.

VIBRATORY HUMMING TECHNIQUE

Similar to the sacred sound vibrations achieved by chanting or breathing "Aum," humming to music can also be utilized to shift your awareness inward and stimulate a state of higher consciousness.

Here's how:

1. Have quiet, spiritually inspiring music playing in the background—music you can easily hum to.

2. As the music is playing, hum to it quietly with your eyes closed.

3. Imagine the vibration of your humming centered in your heart, and try to feel the vibration of your humming there.

4. As you begin to feel the vibration in your heart area, imagine that your heart is sending the vibration into every part of your body.

5. Do this for about three minutes or the length of one piece of music. Then, sit quietly for as long as you wish to meditate, looking into the area of your Third Eye.

CANDLE CONCENTRATION TECHNIQUES

Another simple method of Mystical Meditation involves the use of a candle. This visual technique is especially helpful if you have trouble quieting your mind by practicing any of the previously described methods. What follows are two techniques and how to practice them.

CANDLE CONCENTRATION

1. Place a single candle—preferably white—on a desk or a table.

   - To create an atmosphere that is especially conducive for meditation, place the candle in front of a vase containing one or more flowers, with incense burning in front of the candle.

2. Sit at the desk or table with your spine as straight as possible, and the candle about 12 inches away from you.

3. Light the candle and focus your eyes on the center of the flame.

   - Look intently into the flame with a fixed gaze, and keep your eyes from wandering away from this central point.

   - Remain relaxed, but keep your body as motionless as possible.

   - Breathe deeply.

   - Continue concentrating on the flame as your focused attention helps quiet your mind.

4. After about 5 minutes close your eyes, keeping them centered on the interior of your forehead. You should now perceive the flame as an afterimage in your Third Eye area.

- After closing your eyes, if the flame is not within your inner vision, then reopen your eyes and gaze at the flame's center for another few minutes.

5. When you are successful in keeping the flame within your inner vision, concentrate on it. You have now shifted from an outer point of concentration to an inner one.

    - This inner concentration will continue to still your mind from outer thoughts, and make you more aware of the internal consciousness of your mind.

    - You may notice the image of the flame changing from one color to another, and from one shape to another.

    - Breathe normally and continue your inward gaze until the image of the flame begins to fade away . . . usually in 2 to 3 minutes.

6. When the image of the flame is completely gone, keep your eyes closed and continue to fix your conscious attention on the area of your Third Eye for another 10 minutes or so.

    - It is at this point in your meditation when your mind is the most open to having a higher consciousness contact experience.

7. Finally, open your eyes and watch the flame for a few more minutes, but not so intently.

8. End your meditation by momentarily closing your eyes and mentally saying to yourself:

"Universal Soul . . . Mind . . . Light . . . I thank you."

CANDLE AND SRI YANTRA CONCENTRATION

The sacred geometrical pattern pictured above and on the cover of this book is called the "Sri Yantra." It is a universally recognized pattern representing the totality of reality—both the finite manifest and the infinite unmanifest; the macrocosm of the universe and the microcosm of inner life and being; the divine masculine and the divine feminine.

As a visual point of concentration, this powerful image can help create an inner state of psychic/mystical/spiritual wholeness. And when focused upon it can help lead you into an experience of higher consciousness during meditation.

To practice this concentration technique, do the following:

1. Turn to the Sri Yantra pictured on Page 19. Then, on a desk or table, stand or prop up this book about 2 feet in front of you with the Sri Yantra at eye level.

2. Place a candle—preferably white—in front of the Sri Yantra. Then light the candle and position the flame so it is in front of the center of the Sri Yantra.

3. As you begin your meditation, gaze intently at the center of the Sri Yantra through the burning candle flame.

    o As you do this, concentrate on the thought that all the energies of your mind are coming together into a state of psychic wholeness—a state in which every aspect of your being is one with the Universe.

    o Breathe deeply.

4. After about 5 minutes close your eyes, keeping them centered on the interior of your forehead. You should now perceive the flame as an afterimage in your Third Eye area.

    o After closing your eyes, if the flame is not within your inner vision, then reopen your eyes and gaze at the mandala through the flame for another few minutes.

5. When you are successful in keeping the flame within your inner vision, breathe normally and continue your inward gaze until the image of the flame begins to fade away . . . usually in 2 to 3 minutes.

    o Continue to hold in your mind the idea that you are coming into mystical union with the Universe and All-That-Is.

6. When the image of the flame is completely gone, keep your eyes closed and continue to fix your conscious attention on the area of your Third Eye for another 10 minutes or so.

    o It is at this point in your meditation when your mind is the most open to having a higher consciousness contact experience.

7. Finally, open your eyes and watch the flame for a few more minutes, but not so intently.

8. End your meditation by momentarily closing your eyes and mentally saying to yourself:

"Universal Soul . . . Mind . . . Light . . . I thank you."

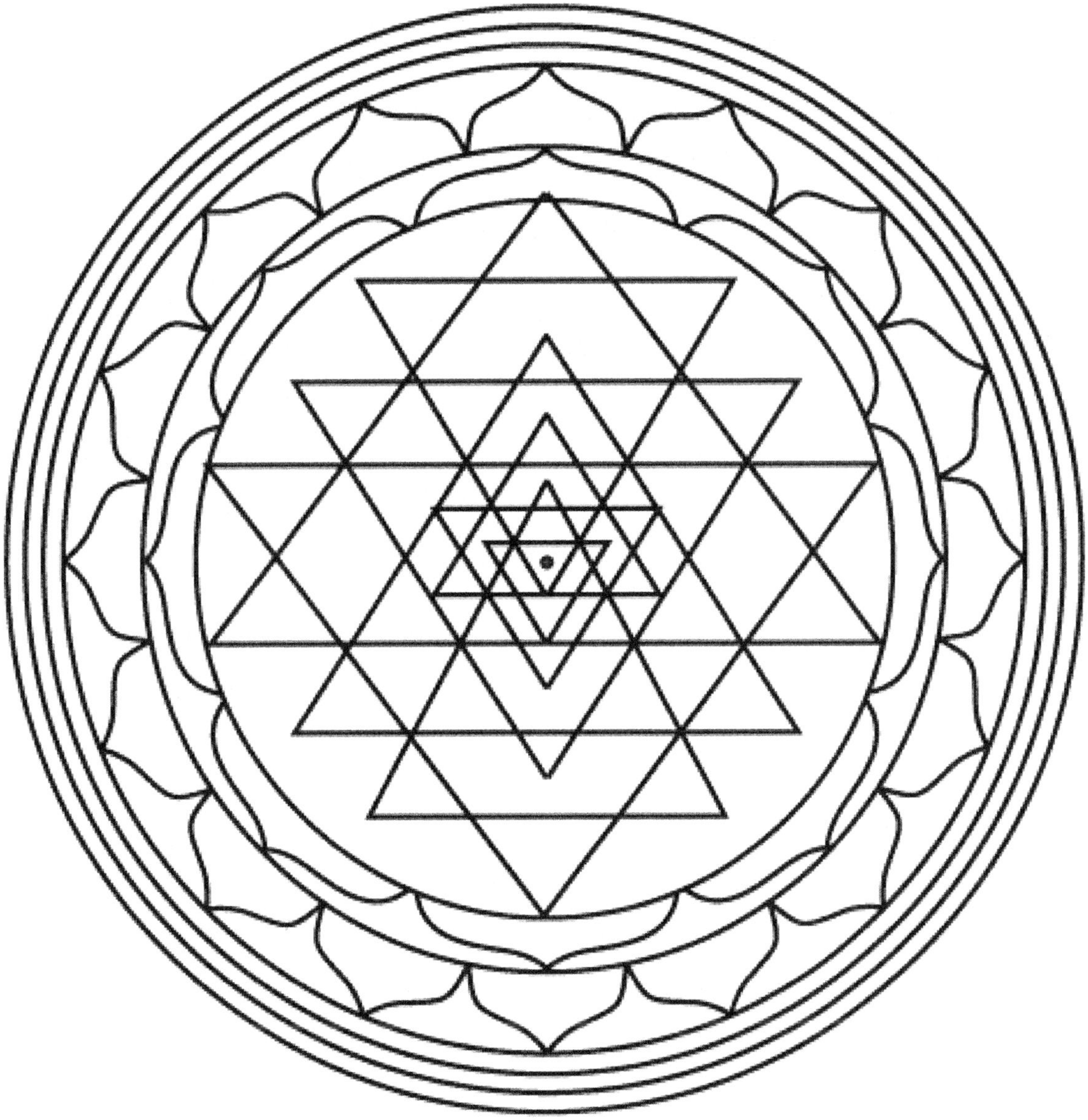

NOTE:

Similar to the Sri Yantra, geometric patterns called "mandalas" (like the ones pictured at the beginning of each major section of this book) can also be used to focus your attention before beginning other methods of meditation, such as measured breathing or the repeating of a mantra. Mandalas can serve as highly effective visual points of concentration with or without the additional use of a candle.

INSTANTANEOUS MEDITATION

Once you have become a fairly practiced meditator, your mind will remember what a meditative state feels like. That memory can be used to usher in a state of meditation at a moment's notice. This can be especially helpful when you feel you need to quickly sublimate a negative thought pattern and reprogram your mind with a positive-thought affirmation, as covered in the upcoming section titled, "Affirmative Meditation."

Here's the technique:

1. Close your eyes.

2. After inhaling, hold back your breath for 3 seconds.

3. During that time, stop all everyday thoughts by holding them back in the same way you are holding your breath.

4. Tell yourself, "As soon as I release my breath, I will recall exactly what it is like—physically and mentally—to be in meditation."

5. As you release your breath, tell yourself, "I am now releasing my breath, body, and mind into meditation."

6. Breathe deeply, much the same as if you were asleep in the middle of the night.

7. If desired, at this point begin to program your mind with one or more positive-thought affirmations.

GUIDED MEDITATION

Another way to practice Mystical Meditation is with the help of a voice that guides you into and through a meditative state. During my many years of research into the nature and dynamics of consciousness, I noticed that whenever I personally guided participants through meditation, they had much better results in experiencing higher states of consciousness. It became apparent that the tonal energies of my voice were taking the higher vibrational energies of my unconscious mind and transferring them to the minds of the participants, helping to stimulate experiences of higher consciousness.

I then began sending participants home with recordings of my guided meditations. The results achieved with those recordings were basically the same as the results achieved when the meditations were experienced in person—higher states of consciousness were stimulated. Eventually, I accumulated 31 different guided meditations that lead people into deeper states of meditation through various forms of visual imagery and spiritual truths gleaned in higher states of consciousness.

THE VOICE OF MEDITATION

All 31 of my guided meditations are now available to you as MP3 Downloads or CDs through www.voiceofmeditation.com. Plus, a link to a free meditation download is always included each week in our University's Email Newsletter. To sign up for this free newsletter, go to www.universityofmetaphysics.com/newsletter.

Most meditations are between 20 and 25 minutes in length, and some are accompanied by music composed especially for those meditations.

To use these recordings, make sure that you first do the following:

1. Take the steps listed in this book under Meditation Preparation.

2. Quiet your mind for several minutes by using any one of these methods:

- With your eyes closed, concentrate on your breathing.
- With your eyes closed, silently repeat a mantra over and over in your mind.
- With your eyes open, gaze intently at a candle flame for a few minutes, then close your eyes and wait for the afterimage to fade.

3. When you feel that your attention is sufficiently focused inwardly, begin to play the recording.

4. While you are listening to the recording, if you begin to notice higher consciousness activity, immediately focus on that instead of the recording. Remember, the purpose of these guided meditations is to help open your mind to an experience of higher consciousness. So, if an experience begins, get involved in that experience and stay with it for as long as it lasts, or for as long as you are comfortable doing so.

AFFIRMATIVE MEDITATION

PRACTICING AFFIRMATIVE MEDITATION

As pointed out in the Introduction, Affirmative Meditation is different from Mystical Meditation. Affirmative Meditation is primarily aimed solely at the *subconscious* level of your mind, which lies between your surface level of consciousness and Universal God-Consciousness at your mind's deepest level.

The purpose is to program the subconscious level of your mind with thoughts that can help you improve your outer life. Said another way, Affirmative Meditation is a highly directed meditation, one that has a specific life-improving goal in mind.

HOW IT WORKS

Since thoughts held in your subconscious mind influence most of your conscious decision-making, it is important that those subconscious thoughts be ones that are beneficial to you. Affirmative Meditation makes use of declarative statements—or affirmations—to program your suggestible subconscious mind with thoughts that are not only positive, but are also founded on spiritual or mystical truths.

These truths help sublimate any negative thought energies in your subconscious mind, and keep that level of your mind aligned with and attuned to the positive Consciousness of the God-Mind deeper within you. In so doing, the surface level of your mind is more open and receptive to the intuitive guidance of your Higher Mind as you go about your daily life.

The end result is that you become a walking demonstration and manifestation of positivity and success as the power of Universal Intelligence is able to work through you and inspire you to live your soul's purpose.

The technique is as follows:

1. Enter a light state of meditation using any of the methods previously described.

2. Begin to concentrate on an affirmation, or series of them.

3. Affirmations should be stated slowly and deliberately, so their meaning is deeply instilled in your subconscious mind. You may want to say the affirmations aloud a few times to begin with, but after that they should be repeated silently in your mind.

4. Continue to focus on your affirmations for the remainder of your meditation period, or for as long as your intuitive sense directs you to.

The best results are achieved when Affirmative Meditation is practiced twice a day—once in the morning and again in the evening. In addition:

- If you feel the need, you can also program your mind at any other time during the day using the Instantaneous Meditation technique.

- You might also want to focus on one or more affirmations right before ending your regular Mystical Meditation practice.

RECOMMENDED AFFIRMATIONS

Here are some powerful affirmations you can use for specific areas of your life that need improvement:

- **FOR HEALTH**

    "In the perfect Mind of the Universe, my body is in complete perfect health already, and I give thanks that so it is."

- **FOR LOVE**

    "In the perfect Mind of the Universe, I already have perfect love with the perfect person for me, and I give thanks that so it is."

- **FOR FINANCIAL PROSPERITY**

    "In the perfect Mind of the Universe, financial prosperity is mine already, and I give thanks that so it is."

- **FOR PEACE**

    "In the perfect Mind of the Universe, my mind and body are filled with peace and relaxation this moment, and I give thanks that so it is."

- **FOR CONFIDENCE**

    "In the perfect Mind of the Universe, my thoughts are inspired this moment for confident self-assurance in every area of my life, and I give thanks that so it is."

- **FOR HIGHER CONSCIOUSNESS**

    "Whenever I meditate, my subconscious mind releases me into the higher consciousness of the perfect Mind of the Universe, and I give thanks that so it is."

- **FOR INTUITIONAL DIRECTION AND INSPIRATION**

    "Every moment of every day, my conscious mind is open to intuitional direction and inspiration from the perfect Mind of the Universe, and I give thanks that so it is."

CREATING YOUR OWN AFFIRMATIONS

There will be many instances in life when you will feel the need to create your own affirmations. Using the preceding affirmations as examples, it is best to follow these guidelines when formulating your wording:

- State your affirmation as if your goal has already been accomplished.

- Use the present tense.

- Be specific about what you are affirming.

- Use positive words.

- Offer thanks.

NOTE:

For more affirmations you can use exactly the way they are worded—or as inspiration for creating your own affirmations—I invite you to look into my book, *Spiritual Mind Power Affirmations*, available in both Paperback and eBook editions. For more information about this book or to order a copy, go to "Dr. Masters' Books" under the "Store" heading at metaphysics.com. Or, contact the University of Metaphysics directly at uom@metaphysics.com.

AFFIRMING HEALTH OF THE BODY

Your body is in a continual state of oneness with the Consciousness of God. In the Mind of God that state is always whole and healthy. If the body appears to need healing, ultimately that healing must come from putting your consciousness back in tune with God's Consciousness.

Every time you meditate you open yourself to the Natural Healing Intelligence of God's Presence within you. Affirmative Meditation makes sure that the subconscious level of your mind is in alignment with that Intelligence, as It automatically directs the energy factors of your body to make any adjustments necessary to maintain or restore health, or intuitively directs you to take additional steps to assist in your healing.

PREPARATION

When it comes to affirming the health or healing of your body, it is helpful to remember that the best results are always achieved when your practice is motivated by the Ultimate Spiritual Level within you—God's Presence. Thus, it is important for you to first establish a sensitivity and responsiveness to that Ultimate Level and Its Healing Power.

This can be accomplished by doing the following, which I call the "Mystical Sensitivity Technique:"

MYSTICAL SENSITIVITY TECHNIQUE

1. First, place your hands over the upper center of your body, next to your heart. This is your Spiritual Center, also called the Heart Chakra. The auric energy emanations of your hands will stimulate the energy currents of this Center into greater activity.

2. Next, close your eyes and imagine that an infinite Field of Light exists within you at this point, even though your physical body is finite.

3. Finally, imagine that this Light, which is the Healing Presence of God, is now flooding all parts of your body. Feel that your entire body has become a Field of Healing God-Light Presence.

MEDITATION

Once you have prepared for your Affirmative Meditation by using the Mystical Sensitivity Technique, use any method you prefer to enter into a meditative state.

When you have reached what you consider to be the high point of your meditation period, feel that your entire psychic-spiritual being is now sensitive and responsive to the Healing Presence of God within you, and that whatever you think or do in this state is within the Grand Energy Vibration of God.

AFFIRMATION

As your subconscious mind vibrates to your positive thoughts and feelings of openness and sensitivity to God's Healing Power, begin to silently repeat this extremely effective affirmation to yourself:

> *"All the energy motions of my body are adjusted to the perfect flow of nature as ordained by God. My body energies are in perfect harmony with the perfect movement of nature throughout the universe."*

Continue to thoughtfully repeat this affirmation to yourself until you feel a peace settle over your body, which is a signal from your intuition that a healing has taken place.

At this point you may end your meditation period and slowly return your consciousness to its normal surface level of awareness.

PSYCHIC-SPIRITUAL TOUCH TECHNIQUE

If there is a specific area of your body you feel needs healing, instead of repeating the above affirmation to yourself—or in addition to doing that—you may want to employ the following Psychic-Spiritual Touch Technique:

1. First, feel as if the total healing spiritual energy presence of your entire body is one with the Natural Healing Power of the Universe, and that this energy is moving into your arms, then down the length of your arms and into your hands and fingers.

2. Now place both hands on the general area of the physical affliction.

3. Mentally form an image in your mind of a Healing White Light entering that area of your body through your hands, healing that area as it does so.

4. Think of this Light as the Healing Presence of God, and therefore perfect and bringing perfection to that part of your body.

5. When intuitively directed to do so, bring your meditation period to a close and slowly return your consciousness to its normal surface level of awareness.

AFFIRMING HEALTH OF THE MIND

Your body is not the only thing that is subject to the Natural Healing Energies of God. Everything in this universe—including your mind with all of its thoughts and resulting emotions—is also held in the Consciousness of God. Therefore, Affirmative Meditation can be used to promote mental healing, as well. The steps to take are the same ones described in the previous chapter:

- Prepare for your Affirmative Meditation by using the Mystical Sensitivity Technique.

- Then use any method you prefer to enter into a meditative state.

- When you have reached what you consider to be the high point of your meditation period, feel that your entire psychic-spiritual being is now sensitive and responsive to the Healing Presence of God within you, and that whatever you think or do in this state is within the Grand Energy Vibration of God.

AFFIRMATION

As your subconscious mind vibrates to your positive thoughts and feelings of openness and sensitivity to God's Healing Power, begin to silently and thoughtfully repeat the following affirmation to yourself:

"At every level of my mind, all negative energies and traumas of the past are sublimated into the Health-Maintaining and Healing Primal Christ-Light Energy of God's Consciousness."

When you are intuitively directed to do so, bring your meditation period to a close and slowly return your consciousness to its normal surface level of awareness.

PSYCHIC-SPIRITUAL TOUCH TECHNIQUE

In combination with an affirmation, the Psychic-Spiritual Touch Technique can also be applied to healing a mind that is suffering from negative subconscious thought patterns.

- As previously described for this technique, send all the healing power of your body down into your hands.

- Place both hands on your forehead and give yourself the following affirmation:

    "The Healing Light Power of God is passing from my hands into my subconscious mind. There, all negative thought pattern energies—like dark shadows—are healed and sublimated into Light and perfect, positive, inspired thinking."

- When intuitively directed to do so, bring your meditation period to a close and slowly return your consciousness to its normal surface level of awareness.

EYE ENERGY TECHNIQUE

An ancient philosopher once wisely said, "The eyes are the window of the soul." Through my own observation, this is an accurate statement. Like any window, the eyes may show what is inside, and, like any window, they may be entered.

So here is an alternate technique for giving yourself an affirmation to heal your subconscious mind of negativity.

1. Stand in front of a mirror and gaze into your own eyes.

    - Feel that your eyes are literally the windows of your soul.

    - Concentrate on this feeling until you are totally absorbed in what you are doing.

2. Feel that whatever you think can now pass behind and beyond your eyes into your mind.

3. Give yourself the following affirmation:

   "Behind my eyes this moment, the God of my mind is healing my subconscious mind of negativity. Behind my eyes is the positive God-Mind Ruler of the Universe, filling my mind with Light."

4. This affirmation may be repeated silently or out loud. Let your intuitive guidance tell you when your subconscious mind has fully accepted this idea.

AFFIRMING FINANCIAL HEALTH AND PROSPERITY

Because absolutely everything in the universe exists in the Mind of God, even circumstances and substances that seem to be outside of you are subject to the Healing Energies of God. That includes your financial situation and your experience of prosperity.

Again, the key to your financial health and prosperity is to make sure that your subconscious mind is aligned with and attuned to the Consciousness of God, which knows only abundance in all things. Affirmative Meditation is a way to make sure that all levels of your mind are open and receptive to receiving God's Abundant Blessings.

PSYCHIC-SPIRITUAL TOUCH TECHNIQUE

In combination with an affirmation, the Psychic-Spiritual Touch Technique is an effective way to help heal the appearance of financial lack or limitation in your life.

1. First, use the method of your choice to enter into a light state of meditation.

2. Then, as previously described for this technique, direct spiritual energy into your hands.

3. Place both hands on something that symbolizes your finances, such as your wallet, checkbook, purse, or pocketbook, and repeat the following affirmation:

    "I direct the psychic-spiritual energy of God's Healing Wholeness into this substance, and only the ideal energy of wholeness, completeness, and thus, prosperity, can abide herein."

4. If you have a stack of unpaid bills, you can do the same, but use this affirmation, instead:

> *"All spiritual channels are open to me for the paying of these bills, and I have faith that in the Mind of God they are already paid."*

5. These affirmations may be repeated silently or out loud. Let your intuitive guidance tell you when it is time to bring your meditation period to a close.

MENTAL MAGNETISM TECHNIQUE

Every physical thing in the universe has an underlying existence as energy. That energy can be acted upon and affected by other energies, such as thought energy. That is the basis for what I call the "Mental Magnetism Technique."

Having both feminine and masculine energy factors within it, your mind can act as a magnet if you regard it as such, enabling you to attract financial increase and abundance to you. It works by drawing upon the psychic energy ideas that underlie the physical existence of money, or something else that you need. This creates unseen but very real psychic energy patterns that act on your behalf, setting up conditions or circumstances in your daily physical life for the receiving of increases in prosperity.

To practice this technique, do the following:

1. For the best results, sit in a comfortable chair.

2. At all times during this technique, regard your mind as a magnet, with the magnetism needed to attract things to you from the psychic ethers.

3. Think of what you are doing as cooperating with the Mind of God to better open your individual mind psychically for a drawing of prosperity to you.

4. Relax for a few moments, entering into a light state of meditation, or deeper.

5. For about one minute, concentrate fully on the idea that your mind is a mental magnet, and that you possess mental, psychic magnetism to draw money and prosperity to you.

6. In your mind, see yourself sitting in the chair you occupy, and imagine that floating through the air toward you is bill after bill of currency. Feel that psychically you are drawing money to yourself.

7. Don't try to figure out by what means it will reach you in physical reality. Rely upon the Universal Mind of God for that.

8. Practice this technique daily for at least three minutes, or longer if your intuition from your Higher Mind seems to be directing you to do so.

LIVING TRULY PROSPEROUSLY

It is important to keep in mind that financial security is only one aspect of prosperity. True prosperity also includes love, health, and happiness. Understanding that prosperity is a natural way of life, made possible by God's Presence within you, is essential. That attitude keeps your mind open to finding and accepting God's bounty.

It is also important to keep your mind open as to how prosperity can manifest in your life. If you need something, it may not come to you through having the money to purchase it. Instead, you may receive it in a trade, or it may be given to you as a gift.

Here's an affirmation to repeat to yourself during meditation:

> *"I totally accept that I am a prosperous person, who accepts abundance and prosperity as a natural way of life, made possible by God's Presence within me."*

AFFIRMING POSITIVE CHANGES IN YOUR LIFE

The Law of the Universe is one of constant change—that is, perpetual self-evolution to ever-greater perfection. The Universe never stands still. It keeps changing and refining itself into a still more positive state.

Since you are a part of the Universe, the laws that operate universally also operate in your life. To stand utterly still, without change of any sort, contradicts the nature of how everything else in the Universe moves and is.

When you understand the universal laws and see how you are either working with them or against them, you then realize how to find greater inner happiness and outer success. In regard to change, the main law to understand is that change represents a natural course of life. Flowing with change, rather than fighting it, creates a state of mind that promotes positive outcomes.

REMOVING FEAR – THE OBSTACLE TO POSITIVE CHANGE

More than any other factor, fear of the unknown is what causes the average person to fight against making any changes in life. In this case, the unknown is what the future might bring if changes of any kind were to occur.

People tend to become accustomed to a particular lifestyle, which translates itself into a false sense of security. By maintaining old, familiar habits and activities, people feel that they are secure. In truth, however, they only have a false sense of security, because the Universe all around them is constantly changing.

To be truly secure, you must trust in the change taking place in the Universe, which, in the final analysis, is always positive in nature. When you practice the principles of metaphysics and meditation, you become sensitive and attuned to the positive energies and vibrations of universal change, which always results in good. By such attunement to the universal vibration of change, fear is removed, and the result is good for the Universe.

LETTING GO TO GO FORWARD

Clinging to the past keeps you living in the past. Yes, there may be many wonderful experiences you have had in your past, and these will always be memories you can reflect on from time to time. However, living mentally in the past by continually referring to the "good old days" does nothing to advance you in the present to positive changes in the future.

Similarly, you may be living in the past by clinging to negative memories, such as hateful feelings about others. Those memories, too, must be released, for they will poison your mind, and because of that, the only thing you can expect in the future is more negativity.

POSITIVE CHANGES REQUIRE POSITIVE NEW MENTAL PATTERNS

Everything begins and is created in the realm of the mind. You cannot think and feel in the same old mental and emotional patterns and expect changes to take place in your life. Therefore, to effect positive changes in your life, you must change your mental thinking patterns—including those at a subconscious level of the mind.

What follows is an affirmative meditation to program your subconscious mind with thoughts that will help keep you open and receptive to positive changes in your life.

AFFIRMATIVE MEDITATION FOR MANIFESTING POSITIVE CHANGES

1. Begin by taking deep, but not forceful, breaths.

   - As you inhale, mentally say to yourself, "I breathe in a positive new future."
   - As you exhale, mentally say to yourself, "I release the past."

2. Repeat this until you feel a deep state of relaxation coming over you.

3. At this point you may discontinue the mental affirmations and move into an even deeper state of meditation. Or, you can continue to program your subconscious mind by silently repeating to yourself one or more of the following affirmations:

   "Positive change in my life is mine already through my attunement to the Positive Universal Law of Change."

   "My mind vibrates to the positive changes in the Universe in my individual life."

   "As the Universe creates positive new changes, I create positive new changes in my individual life via the Universe working through my mind."

   "My subconscious mind is open to impressions from my God-Mind for the creation of positive new mental patterns for effective changes in my life."

   "I have forgiven all and everyone in my life; therefore, my mind is free to move into new positive changes."

4. When you are intuitively directed to do so, bring your meditation period to a close and slowly return your consciousness to its normal surface level of awareness.

GUIDELINES FOR BRINGING ABOUT POSITIVE CHANGES

Beginning with maintaining a positive mental attitude, here is a list of other things you can do to bring about positive changes in your life:

- **EACH DAY, PUT YOURSELF INTO A FEARLESS STATE** by attuning your thinking and soul to the positive changes of the Universe, and by accepting the beautiful truth that your life is under the rule of the Universal Law of Change. Do this by maintaining a positive conscious and subconscious mental attitude, and by entering into a state of deep meditation daily.

- **MAKE A LIST** of things you would like to see changed for the better in your life, and truly believe that your Universal God-Mind-Self can and will actually materialize them.

- **RELEASE YOURSELF FROM ALL PAST NEGATIVE FEELINGS** about anyone and anything. Understand why others were as they were, and ask the Universal Healing Presence within you to help you forgive and release them from your subconscious mind.

- **MINIMIZE CONTACT** with those people who fit your old way of thinking. Mix more with people who are looking to a positive future, and who are building for it in their minds now.

- **DON'T MIX WITH PEOPLE WHO CARRY GRUDGES** and who are thus living in the past. Associate instead with those who have the spiritual understanding to forgive.

- **EACH DAY VISUALIZE THE WAY YOU WANT TO LIVE**, doing the things you want to do. If you make something a psychic reality in your mind, the psychic vibrations of your mind will enter into the Universal Mind and draw what you want to you.

- **BELIEVE IN YOURSELF** by believing in the Universe within you. Know and accept that the Presence of Universal Mind within you is, in truth, the Creative Power of Life, or God.

- **LOOK TO YOUR INNER, HIGHER UNIVERSAL MIND TO GUIDE YOU** and give you the answers as to how to go about making positive changes in your life. These answers may come to you in dreams, inspirations, or intuitive hunches. The main thing you can be sure of is that they will come if you maintain a positive conscious and subconscious attitude, and if you meditate daily.

SLEEP PROGRAMMING

A particularly good time to program your mind with positive-thought affirmations is right before you go to sleep at night. This is because your conscious mind will soon be completely quiet and still, while your subconscious mind will continue to be active; therefore, whatever it is you suggest to your mind will have plenty of time to become deeply seated in your subconscious.

The technique is to combine deliberate breathing with a positive thought that you silently think to yourself over and over again. For example, as you inhale you might think, "While I sleep," and as you exhale, "my body is healing." You would continue to repeat this thought with every breath until you begin to fall asleep.

Optionally, in sync with your breathing, you might choose to slowly and silently read to yourself all of the recommended affirmations listed below, or some of them.

RECOMMENDED AFFIRMATIONS

YOUR PURPOSE	INHALATION SUGGESTION	EXHALATION SUGGESTION
PHYSICAL HEALING	*While I sleep . . .*	*my body is healed.*
PEACE	*As I sleep . . .*	*peace fills me.*
SELF-DIRECTION	*While I sleep . . .*	*I am directed.*
CONFIDENCE	*As I sleep . . .*	*I am one with a Higher Power.*

AWARENESS	*While I sleep . . .*	*awareness awakens in me.*
MATERIAL NEEDS	*As I sleep . . .*	*I am supplied.*
PROSPERITY	*While I sleep . . .*	*I am prospered.*
CREATIVITY	*As I sleep . . .*	*creativity surfaces.*
LOVE	*While I sleep . . .*	*I attract love.*
SECURITY	*As I sleep . . .*	*my needs are met.*
CAREER	*While I sleep . . .*	*my career improves.*
OPPORTUNITIES	*As I sleep . . .*	*opportunities are drawn to me.*
ASSERTIVENESS	*While I sleep . . .*	*my Higher Mind asserts me.*
POTENTIALS	*As I sleep . . .*	*my potentials are realized.*
CAPACITY	*While I sleep . . .*	*my capacities expand.*

COMMUNICATING	*As I sleep . . .*	*expression fills me.*
SPIRITUAL AWARENESS	*While I sleep . . .*	*my soul blossoms as a flower.*
ONENESS WITH GOD	*As I sleep . . .*	*I am One with God.*
WISDOM	*While I sleep . . .*	*Infinite Mind and I are One.*

SUGGESTIVE SELF-HYPNOSIS

PRACTICING SUGGESTIVE SELF-HYPNOSIS

Affirmative Meditation is not the only way to program your mind with beneficial thoughts. You may also employ Suggestive Self-Hypnosis. Affirmative Meditation and Self-Hypnosis are very similar in their initial stages of practice. Both involve a combination of relaxation and concentration. And both are directed at the subconscious level of the mind—the level where the mind is the most suggestible to what it is being told.

The main difference is that Self-Hypnosis employs more mechanical means—or hypnotic "tools"—to induce a suggestible state of mind, such as gazing at the image of a spinning spiral; watching a pendulum swinging back and forth in front of your eyes; or staring intently at a candle flame—similar to the Candle Concentration Techniques described previously, but more involved.

As many people do, you may find that using Self-Hypnotic procedures such as these is an easier way to still your restless mind—to put your surface level of consciousness "to sleep," so to speak. When that level of your mind is quiet, the subconscious level of your mind can be more easily reached, and then programmed with positive suggestions or affirmations to help you successfully deal with problems or issues you may be experiencing in your outer life.

GUIDELINES FOR INDUCING SELF-HYPNOSIS

Inducing self-hypnosis not only employs the use of hypnotic tools, but also involves induction suggestions that can be quite lengthy and repetitive in the way they are worded. Because of that, it is recommended that you use a device to pre-record the induction, and then play it back to yourself, as if you were listening to a guided meditation.

Additional guidelines include these:

- If you pre-record your hypnotic induction, breathe heavily into the microphone as you record.

- If desired, experiment with playing soft melodies in the background as you record your induction.

- If you do not pre-record your induction, do not read the suggestions to yourself as you induct. Instead, memorize the basic wording of the induction. It does not have to be word for word; use words that are comfortable and natural to you, as long as the ideas that you are conveying to yourself remain the same.

- Before beginning the self-hypnosis session, fully relax using measured breathing or some other relaxation exercise.

- Do not hurry. Take your time and drag out induction suggestions by thinking about them thoroughly as you say them to yourself.

- Attempt to feel each induction suggestion taking effect as you are thinking it, such as when you are imagining your arms, legs, or body getting heavy.

- Continuously repeat the induction suggestions to yourself until you feel their mental-physical manifestation.

- After you have brought about a fair degree of hypnosis, concentrate your suggestions on deepening the hypnotic state. For example, "I am now going still deeper and deeper into sleep." Or, "I am drifting further and further still into hypnotic sleep."

- If you are giving yourself more than one self-improvement suggestion or affirmation during the self-hypnotic period, deepen the hypnotic level after each suggestion is made.

AWAKENING PROCEDURE

When you are ready to end your self-hypnotic session, say the following to yourself:

"In a few moments, I will begin to count to five.

One . . . My mind is awakening from self-hypnosis.

Two . . . I am relaxed . . . peaceful . . . calm.

Three . . . My eyes are beginning to open now. At the count of five they will be fully open . . . and I will be fully awake.

Four . . . I am almost completely awake now. The moment I say 'Five' I will be completely awake . . . wide awake. I will feel completely refreshed and relaxed.

Five! . . . I am awake now . . . completely awake . . . wide awake . . . completely relaxed and refreshed."

NOTE:
The words "sleep" and "awake" are not to be taken literally in an induction. They are merely symbolic of a conscious mind that has been stilled—as in sleep—and then returned to state of present moment awareness.

HYPNOTIC PENDULUM TECHNIQUE

This technique for self-hypnosis has been placed first in this section of the book because it uses a hypnotic tool that you are probably already familiar with—that of a pendulum swinging back and forth in front of the eyes.

The ideal pendulum should be comprised of an 8-inch chain (or string) with a small object at the end of the chain that can catch and reflect light. If possible, that object should be a round ball made of crystal, glass, or plastic. However, other shapes and materials will also work if they contain highly reflective facets. If you can't find a pendulum similar to this for sale, you may be able to make one yourself out of an inexpensive necklace and pendant.

PREPARATION

Hold the chain between your thumb and index finger, so that the crystal ball is about two inches in front of your face, at a level directly in line with the bridge of your nose.

With a small movement of your hand, start the crystal ball swinging from side to side in front of your eyes. The best results are obtained if the crystal is kept from swinging no more than about a half-inch in either direction, right or left. Just a very slight swinging motion is what you want.

As the crystal ball swings, have your eyes follow its movement, keeping your eyes looking into the center of it.

Watch this back-and-forth movement for a few moments, and then give yourself the following induction suggestions:

INDUCTION

"As I watch the crystal ball, I am becoming relaxed and drowsy.

My eyes are tiring . . . growing tired watching.

> **My eyelids are beginning to flutter . . . beginning to flutter.**
>
> **My eyelids feel very heavy now . . . very heavy.**
>
> **It is becoming harder to watch the swinging pendulum.**
>
> **It would be easier for me to close my eyes and fall into a hypnotic sleep.**
>
> **My eyelids are so heavy now . . . so much wanting to close that I may fall into a pleasant . . . restful . . . sound . . . hypnotic sleep."**

When your eyelids have become so heavy that you can no longer keep them open comfortably, let them close and give yourself the following suggestion:

> **"As I close my eyes, it is a signal that I am falling into a sound . . . deep . . . hypnotic sleep."**

At this stage of the induction, you may want to test yourself to ascertain if you are in a truly hypnotic state. Later in this book you will find several testing methods described in the section titled, "Testing Self-Hypnosis."

When you believe that you are, indeed, in a hypnotic state of mind, that is the time to program your subconscious with self-improvement suggestions, such as:

> *"I always make healthy meal choices."*
>
> *"No matter what is going on around me, I feel peaceful."*

Or, you may impress upon your subconscious mind affirmations, such as:

> *"Every moment of every day I am open and receptive to intuitive guidance, and I give thanks that so it is."*

"I am already a prosperous person, because prosperity is a natural way of life made possible by God's Presence within me . . . and so it is!"

When you are ready to end your self-hypnotic session, go through the Awakening Procedure previously described.

TOTAL BODY RELAXATION TECHNIQUE

As you know, there is a very close connection between your mind and body. It is no surprise, then, that relaxing your body can also lead to relaxing your mind. And when your mind is relaxed, it is easier to induce a hypnotic state of consciousness. That is the basis for this particular self-hypnotic induction.

Because of the length of this induction, you will most likely want to pre-record it. It also includes the use of a hypnotic mandala.

PREPARATION

Turn to the mandala pictured on Page 59. Then, on a desk or table, stand or prop up this book about 2 feet in front of you with the mandala at eye level.

As you begin your meditation, gaze intently at the center of the mandala. Then, after a few moments, give yourself the following induction suggestions:

INDUCTION

"I now relax every muscle in my body. I relax the toes of my right foot. I let them go limp, limp, heavy and relaxed. I let this relaxation creep up through the ball, arch, and heel of the foot . . . all the way to the ankle . . . so my right foot is completely relaxed, relaxed and heavy, heavy and limp.

Now I relax the toes on my left foot . . . the toes, the ball, the arch, and the heel. My left foot is completely relaxed, relaxed and limp, limp and heavy. Both feet are now completely relaxed, relaxed and heavy.

I let this heaviness creep up the calf of my right leg . . . so I am now completely relaxed from the tip of my right toes to the knee. Now I let the left calf relax in the same manner so that both feet and legs are completely relaxed up to the knees.

Now the relaxation extends up through the large muscles of the right leg and thigh, so that my whole right leg is relaxed up to the hip. Now I let my left thigh also relax, so that my feet and legs are heavy, heavy and relaxed, loose and limp. So relaxed, so limp, so heavy.

My eyes are very heavy now, so drowsy and so sleepy. It is becoming difficult for me to keep my eyes open. Soon they will become so relaxed and so sleepy that they will close of their own accord. They are becoming so drowsy and so sleepy with the gazing . . . gazing . . . gazing.

Now I relax the fingers of my right hand. I feel them getting limp and heavy and relaxed. I feel my right hand relaxing more and more . . . getting limper and limper, heavier and heavier. Now the fingers of my left hand are letting go completely, all muscles relaxing . . . the fingers getting heavy, limp, relaxed. The left hand is becoming relaxed and heavy.

Now I let that feeling flow up the arms. The right forearm relaxed . . . the left forearm relaxed . . . the right upper arm relaxed . . . the left upper arm relaxed . . . both hands and both arms are relaxed and heavy and limp all the way up to the shoulders.

By this time I might notice a slight, pleasant tingling in my toes and fingers. If so, this feeling will increase until I am completely bathed in a pleasant glow of utter relaxation.

Now I am going to relax my body. The hips, the large back muscles, the abdomen, the chest muscles, and the shoulders will relax at once. I am going to take three deep breaths. Each time I exhale I notice the body relaxing more and more. With the third deep breath comes a complete and utter relaxation of my entire body.

- Now I breathe slowly in . . . in . . . in . . . in a full, deep breath.
  I breathe out and relax completely.

- Now a deeper breath in . . . in . . . in . . . in.
  I breathe out and relax completely.

- Now the last time . . . in . . . in . . . in . . . in . . . in.
  Now out and completely relaxed.

Now I breathe slowly, gently, deeply as a sleeper breathes. Every muscle in my chest, shoulders, back, abdomen, and hips is relaxed, and my body is heavy, heavy, heavy and limp. I am now completely relaxed. My arms are relaxed, my legs are relaxed, my body is relaxed.

My eyes are so sleepy, so drowsy. The lids are so heavy. All the muscles in my neck are now beginning to relax. My head feels so heavy as the muscles release their tension. I let my jaw muscles relax so that my teeth do not quite touch . . . jaw muscles completely relaxed. I let all the muscles of the face and scalp relax completely. So limp, so heavy, so perfectly relaxed.

Now I will relax my eye muscles. I am going to start counting.

- On the first count, I close my eyes.
- On the second count, I open them with my attention still focused on the mandala.
- On the third count, I close them.
- On the fourth count, I open them.
- I continue on and on in this manner.

Each time my eyes open I have my attention fixed closely on the mandala. I find that each time I close my eyes they want to stay closed. Each time I open them it will be more difficult to do so, each time more difficult than the previous time . . . much more difficult. Soon my eyelids will stick so tightly that it will be impossible to open them. Soon they will stay closed."

When you can no longer keep your eyelids open comfortably, let them close and give yourself the following suggestion:

" I am now falling into a sound . . . deep . . . hypnotic sleep."

At this stage of the induction, you may want to test yourself to ascertain if you are in a truly hypnotic state. Later in this book you will find several testing methods described in the section titled, "Testing Self-Hypnosis."

When you believe that you are, indeed, in a hypnotic state of mind, it is time to program your subconscious mind with self-improvement suggestions or affirmations.

When you wish to end your self-hypnotic period, use the Awakening Procedure described previously.

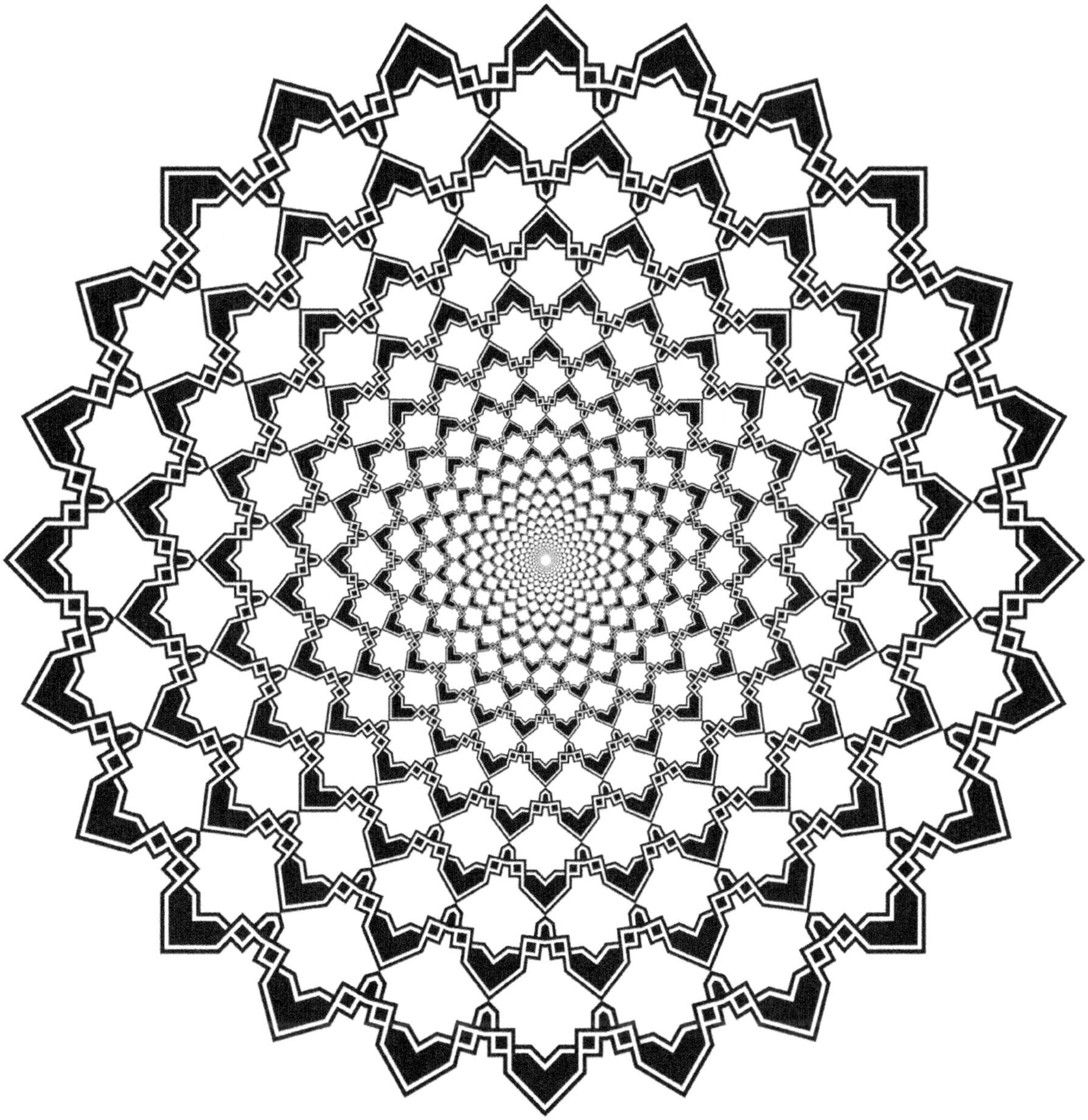

DEEP SLEEP CANDLE TECHNIQUE

I have successfully used this technique to bring about a very deep state of self-hypnosis. The basis for this technique is the use of repetition to create a state of monotony, which tends to wear the mind down, thus minimizing and/or eliminating conscious resistance.

In this case, the repetition is the continual opening and closing of the eyes in conjunction with hypnotic suggestions. This repetition results in a psycho-physical condition that greatly facilitates a total letting go into a deep self-hypnotic state. The technique is as follows:

- Place a lit candle in front of you, with the flame about 12 inches away from you at eye level.

- For about one minute, stare intently at the flame.

- Let your breathing become heavy and deep, as it is when you are asleep at night.

- With your eyes open, say the word "SLEEP" out loud.

- Immediately after you have said the word "SLEEP," close your eyes and say the words "DEEP SLEEP" out loud.

- As soon as you have said the words "DEEP SLEEP," open your eyes and say the word "SLEEP" out loud.

Continue on and on in this manner until you begin achieving the hypnotic indicators below:

HYPNOTIC INDICATORS

- Difficulty in opening the eyes with each repetition

- Heaviness of the eyelids

- Growing difficulty in coordinating the words "SLEEP" and "DEEP SLEEP" in conjunction with the opening and closing of the eyes

- A slurring of the words as they are said out loud

- A very tired feeling in which you want very much to stop and close your eyes

When this happens, do close your eyes and let yourself go into a deep state of hypnotic sleep. At this point you can program your subconscious mind with self-improvement suggestions or affirmations.

When you wish to end your self-hypnotic period, use the Awakening Procedure described previously.

WAKING (EYES OPEN) SELF-HYPNOSIS

If you are fairly accomplished at inducing self-hypnosis, it may be possible for you to maintain a hypnotic state with your eyes open. This can be especially helpful if you want to program your subconscious mind with self-improvement suggestions or affirmations that you would prefer to read because of their length.

Here are the specific instructions for achieving a state of waking (eyes open) hypnosis, which requires testing your hypnotic state:

1. Induce hypnosis using the technique that works best for you, closing your eyes as you enter into hypnotic sleep.

2. Give yourself a suggestibility test, preferably either the Handclasp Test or the Rigid Arm Test (described in the section of this book titled, "Testing Self-Hypnosis").

3. Pay particular attention to the test that you give yourself.

    - Notice the degree of difficulty experienced in trying to unclasp your hands or bend your arm.
    - Make a mental note of it.

4. After the test, use the Test Suggestion Removal process (described in the section of this book titled, "Testing Self-Hypnosis") to both remove the test suggestion and re-deepen your hypnotic state.

5. Following your re-deepening, give yourself this suggestion:

    "I am going to open my eyes in a moment. The moment I open them, it will be a signal to go into a deeper self-hypnotic state . . . even though I have opened my eyes."

6. Repeat this suggestion to yourself a few times until you feel that your subconscious mind has thoroughly accepted it.

7. Let your eyes open. As they open, reinforce your prior suggestions by telling yourself:

   "As I now open my eyes, I am entering into a still deeper self-hypnotic state."

8. With your eyes now open, repeat to yourself a few times:

   "Though my eyes are open, I remain in a hypnotic state."

9. Now give yourself the Handclasp Test or Rigid Arm Test, or both. If you succeed with these tests, then you have achieved waking hypnosis!

10. You can judge the depth of this waking hypnosis state by comparing (via remembering) the difficulty you had in unclasping your hands or bending your arm when your eyes were closed.

11. Once again use the Test Suggestion Removal process to both remove the test suggestion and further re-deepen your hypnotic state.

12. When you are ready to end your waking (eyes open) self-hypnotic session, let your eyes close once more and then go through the standard Awakening Procedure.

SELF-HYPNOTIC MEDITATION

PRACTICING SELF-HYPNOTIC MEDITATION

Although Self-Hypnosis is primarily practiced for the purpose of programming the subconscious mind with life-improving thoughts, it can also be used to experience a higher state of consciousness—that same higher state experienced in Mystical Meditation where you are in contact with Universal Consciousness, or the Mind of God. I call this merger of self-hypnosis and meditation, "Self-Hypnotic Meditation."

The technique is basically quite simple. Once you feel you are in a suggestible state of mind through self-hypnosis, you simply suggest to your subconscious mind that you are ready to move into a deeper meditative state that is conducive to an experience of higher consciousness. Literally, you would suggest something to your subconscious mind similar to this:

"I am now moving into a deeper meditative state."

"I now open myself to an experience of higher consciousness."

At that point you allow yourself to move deeper and deeper into meditation until you either have a contact experience of some kind, or you are inwardly directed to bring your self-hypnotic meditation period to a close.

What follows in this section of the book are two additional techniques using self-hypnotic inductions for a meditative purpose.

MYSTICAL SELF-HYPNOSIS

This self-hypnotic induction not only guides you into a state of deep hypnotic sleep, but the suggestions themselves simultaneously open you to an experience of God's Presence within you. Because of the length of this induction, you will most likely want to pre-record it.

INDUCTION

"I am relaxing my physical body and mind identity.

My physical body and mind identity are relaxing.

My human self is filling with relaxation.

Soon, my physical and mental self will be asleep.

I am giving up the power of my human self and its will.

My human identity is relaxing . . . ready to fall asleep.

As soon as my human self goes to sleep, there will be no other identity within me but that of the Divine Presence of God.

My physical self is giving up its identity . . . is falling fast asleep . . . so that my awareness may rest in God.

Every muscle and nerve of my physical body is relaxed and at ease . . . so also is my earthly mind.

My body is growing heavy and sleepy . . . as a pleasant feeling of God's Presence is awakening in me.

My legs feel very heavy . . . as a pleasant feeling of God's Presence is awakening in me.

My head and eyes and my entire physical self and earthly mind are heavy and deep with relaxation . . . drifting effortlessly into sleep and into submission to the Divine Consciousness of my soul in God.

The more my eyes close, the more that which surrounds me physically seems distant . . . and as the distance to my physical surroundings increases, so it is being replaced by the Divine Light of God's Presence.

My entire body, mind, and will are relaxing as an inflow of God's Presence is awakening in me with each and every breath I take.

My eyes are heavy now . . . very heavy . . . and my earthly self is relaxed and ready to yield itself to sleep.

Soon I will close my eyes, and when I do my human self will yield itself to sleep and my soul will be awake in Infinite Universal Presence.

Now my eyes are closed . . . so let my earthly identity sleep . . . so let me awaken to Infinity within me . . . so sleep earthly self . . . so awaken Divine Self . . . so be it.

My earthly, worldly identity sleeps now . . . sleeps . . . sleeps . . . all the time into still deeper and more relaxed sleep . . . while a sense of Cosmic Consciousness in God continues to awaken within, throughout, and about me . . . all the time awakening.

The deeper my earthly self sleeps, the more awake is my soul to the Cosmic Consciousness of God's Consciousness in mine.

Deeper . . . deeper . . . deeper into sleep is my earthly self enters.

The deeper into sleep my earthly self enters, the more the Cosmos awakens in God's Presence within me.

My earthly self is going deeper to sleep . . . and my earthly will and my earthly mind are given to God.

Let the Power that now controls me be only the creative flow of Cosmic Soul Consciousness in God.

More and more as I sleep, I am yielding my whole being to God and to the Eternal Heartbeat of Nature and the Universe . . . a Heartbeat . . . a Presence . . . flowing through my consciousness, merging with me from within, and surrounding me with Divine Light as my physical body sleeps.

My earthly self now falls even deeper into sleep, and as this happens, the Cosmic Consciousness of God flows increasingly through me.

Deep sleep . . . sound . . . spiritual sleep.

I have given up my earthly self, my worldly self and will.

The Cosmic Consciousness of the Universe in God flows through every atom of my body.

I now merge into God and Eternity within myself. All the beauties of God and my soul fill me with a vision of Divine Peace, Love, and Eternal Life."

At this point allow yourself some time to remain in blissful Oneness with God's Presence. When you are ready to awaken to your outer, surface level of consciousness, say the following to yourself:

AWAKENING

"When I awaken I will be thoroughly relaxed in body, and I will remain under the influence of the Perfect Divine Movement of all the Universe in every atom of my body and in every internal organ.

My mind will be completely refreshed, and although wide awake, I will remain under the Direction of the Infinite Will of the Universe and Life Eternal . . . under the Direction of God.

At the count of five, my earthly self will be wide awake, but it will continue in body and mind to live, to think, and to breathe in the Perfection of God.

One.

Two . . . My mind is now returning to the external.

Three . . . My mind is now coming closer to my external daily consciousness.

Four . . . My mind is right at the edge of opening to my external consciousness.

Five! . . . My eyes are open, and I am once again wide awake to the world around me, with a continuous sense of the world within me."

DEEP SLEEP CANDLE TECHNIQUE II

This is a variation of the Deep Sleep Candle Technique described in the section on Suggestive Self-Hypnosis. Here you will be utilizing different suggestion words in place of the words "SLEEP" and "DEEP SLEEP." The idea is to induce a state of self-hypnosis and—at the very same time—program your subconscious mind with suggestions you want your mind to accept.

What follows are sets of suggestion words listed in two columns. The first column is for programming your mind for basic self-improvement. The second column is for programming your mind for more spiritually based improvement, or for releasing your mind into meditation and a higher state of consciousness.

SELF-IMPROVEMENT	HIGHER CONSCIOUSNESS
Peace – Deep Peace	Mind – Awareness Expanding
Calm – Complete Calm	Consciousness – Ever Awakening
Love – Perfect Love	Soul – Ever Revealing
Warmth – Radiant Warmth	Oneness – With God
Magnetism – Vibrant Magnetism	Synthesis – Inner Unity
Youth – New Youth	Christ – Divine Self
Complexion – Cell Rejuvenation	Buddha – Universal Self
Health – Perfect Health	Krishna – God Self
Direction – Intuitive Direction	Being – Divine Harmony

Help – Divine Help	Reality – Inner Consciousness
Supply – Universal Supply	Awareness – Inwardly Unfolding
Discipline – Is Mine	Light – Total Union
Control – Is Mine	Identity – Inner Expansion
Happiness – Inwardly Mine	Unity – One Within
Power – God Within	Karma – Divine Freedom

TESTING SELF-HYPNOSIS

PUTTING SELF-HYPNOSIS TO THE TEST

At some point you might want to put self-hypnosis to the test—that is, you might want to test yourself to see if you truly are in a hypnotic state. What follows in this section are a number of tests you can use. All of these particular tests involve the use of a body part.

For instance, in one test you give yourself the hypnotic suggestion that you cannot bend one of your arms. It is important, of course, to remove that suggestion after the test. To make sure that the suggestion is completely removed, I highly recommend that you prepare in advance for this with the following Test Suggestion Removal process:

TEST SUGGESTION REMOVAL

For at least three days before giving yourself any test suggestion involving any part of your body, give yourself the following suggestion while you are in a self-hypnotic state:

> "Any time I test my self-hypnotic state using any part of my body, I will return that part of my body back to its normal state by using the following words:
>
> Back to normal . . .
> All test suggestions on this part of my body are removed . . .
> It is completely back to normal."

It is very important to follow up the above test removal suggestion with this additional suggestion:

> "As soon as this part of my body is back to normal, it will act as a signal for me to go into a still deeper state of self-hypnosis."

EYELID CLOSURE TEST

This is the most commonly used of all tests to ascertain whether or not a state of hypnosis has been achieved. It is the perfect test simply because closing the eyes is a typical part of the standard techniques for inducing self-hypnosis.

SUGGESTIVE WORDING

For the express purpose of testing your hypnotic state, here is some recommended wording you can use as part of your self-hypnotic induction:

"My eyes are beginning to feel tired. My eyelids feel heavy . . . very heavy.

My eyelids are fluttering . . . as they continue to tire. My eyelids are becoming heavier . . . and heavier.

My eyelids are becoming watery. I can hardly keep my eyes open. I just want to close my eyes . . . to close my eyes . . . to fall fast asleep."

As soon as you no longer can keep your eyes open comfortably, close them while telling yourself:

"I am now entering into a deep, hypnotic sleep.

My eyelids are closed tightly together . . . tightly together. They are stuck together . . . stuck together . . . locked together.

When I count to three, no matter how hard I try to open them, my eyes will remain closed. The harder I try to open them, the more they will stick and lock tightly together.

One . . . My eyelids are stuck tightly together.

Two . . . My eyelids are glued tightly together, and I cannot open them. I cannot open them.

Three . . . My eyelids are locked completely together . . . locked completely together."

Now, keep repeating the words "locked tightly" as you try to open your eyes.

If you cannot open your eyes, the test is a success and you are, indeed, in a deep, hypnotic state.

Now, bring your eyelids back to their normal closed but relaxed state with these words from the Text Suggestion Removal process:

**"Back to normal . . .
All test suggestions on this part of my body are removed . . .
It is completely back to normal."**

And immediately follow this with:

"As soon as this part of my body is back to normal, it is a signal for me to go into a still deeper state of self-hypnosis."

RIGID ARM TEST

Once you have induced a state of self-hypnosis, do the following:

- Extend one arm to the side.
- Clench your fist tightly.
- Lock your arm stiffly at the elbow.
- Think of your arm as an inflexible mass, as stiff and rigid as a bar of steel.
- Give yourself the hypnotic suggestion that you will begin to mentally count to five, and that when you reach the count of five, it will be impossible for you to bend your arm.

SUGGESTIVE WORDING

"My arm is stiff and rigid. I will begin to mentally count to five. With each count my arm will be more and more rigid. When I reach the count of five it will be impossible for me to bend my arm.

One . . . My arm is as stiff and rigid as a bar of steel.

Two . . . My arm is tightening . . . tightening . . . tightening.

Three . . . My arm is rigid . . . stiff . . . stiff . . . rigid.

Four . . . My arm is completely locked at the elbow . . . as unbendable as a bar of steel. When I next count to five, it will be impossible for me to bend my arm. It will be stiff, rigid, frozen . . . as a bar of steel!

Five . . . I try to bend my arm now, but I find it impossible to bend, as it is as stiff and rigid as a bar of steel!"

A few seconds of trying to bend your arm unsuccessfully is sufficient for this test. Conclude as follows:

"At the count of three, I will once again be able to bend my arm easily. One . . . Two . . . Three!"

After you have completed the count and bent your arm, use the Test Suggestion Removal process to both remove the test suggestion and further re-deepen your hypnotic state.

HANDCLASP TEST

Once you have induced a state of self-hypnosis, do the following:

- On your lap, fold both of your hands together, with your fingers interlocked and your palms together. (Alternatively, you can lock your hands together behind your head.)

- Begin to imagine that your hands are locking more and more tightly together.

- Give yourself the hypnotic suggestion that you will begin to mentally count to five, and that when you reach the count of five, it will be impossible for you to unlock your hands.

SUGGESTIVE WORDING

"My hands are locked tightly together. I will begin to mentally count to five. With each count my hands will lock even more tightly together. When I reach the count of five it will be impossible for me to separate my hands.

One . . . My hands are locking more tightly together.

Two . . . My palms can only press towards each other.

Three . . . My fingers are frozen together.

Four . . . My hands cannot separate when I say FIVE, because they are locked tightly . . . tightly . . . together.

Five . . . I try to separate my hands now, but I cannot, even though I try!"

A few seconds of trying to separate your hands unsuccessfully is sufficient for this test. Conclude as follows:

> **"At the count of three, I will once again be able to separate my hands. One . . . Two . . . Three!"**

After you have completed the count and separated your hands, use the Test Suggestion Removal process to both remove the test suggestion and further re-deepen your hypnotic state.

HAND LEVITATION TEST

Once you have induced a state of self-hypnosis, do the following:

- Have your writing hand resting comfortably on the arm of the chair you are sitting in.

- Place your mind on your entire arm for a few moments. At first, your arm may seem heavy due to the effect of your self-hypnotic state.

- Begin to imagine that the heaviness is leaving your arm.

- Give yourself the following hypnotic suggestions:

SUGGESTIVE WORDING

"My arm is growing light . . . lighter . . . and lighter. All the weight of my arm is going . . . going . . . gone. My arm feels weightless.

My arm is so light that soon my hand will begin to float upward toward my face.

My arm is so light that my hand wants to float up towards my face and touch it. My hand wishes to float up towards my face and touch it."

Make no voluntary effort to move your hand towards your face. Let your subconscious mind move your hand.

Do not become impatient if your hand does not begin to move immediately. It should eventually lift upward towards your face.

If your hand does not lift towards your face within about five minutes, discontinue this test and try a different test.

If the test succeeds, rest your hand back on the arm of your chair and conclude as follows:

> **"At the count of three, my arm will regain its normal weight. One . . . Two . . . Three!"**

After you have completed the count use the Test Suggestion Removal process to both remove the test suggestion and further re-deepen your hypnotic state.

MORE TESTS AND TOOLS

CHEVREUL PENDULUM TEST

Another aspect of putting self-hypnosis to the test is testing to see if a self-betterment suggestion you gave yourself in a previous session has truly taken root in your subconscious mind. The Chevreul Pendulum Test is an excellent way to find out, because you are actually communicating directly with your subconscious mind.

This test can not only help you determine if your subconscious mind has accepted a suggestion, but it can also be used to analyze your inner resistance to taking suggestions, and/or to ascertain your true motives, aims, and goals.

PREPARATION

For this test you will need a pendulum similar to the one described in the Hypnotic Pendulum Technique. Like that one, it should be comprised of an 8-inch-long chain (or string) with a small object at the end of the chain. However, the object does not have to be round or reflective.

You will also need a piece of paper with the image of a circle, which has been divided into four parts by two crossed lines. For your convenience, you will find one on Page 92, which you can either use or copy.

You will be questioning your subconscious mind, seeking "Yes" or "No" answers, with two alternative answers of "I don't know" or "I don't wish to answer."

PROCEDURE

- Hold the chain or string between your thumb and index finger, with your elbow resting on a table, desk, arm of a chair, or on your knee.

- Have your pendulum hanging freely, directly one inch above the circle at the point where the two lines cross.

- You will receive answers to questions you pose to your subconscious mind through one of four basic movements:

    1. Back and forth along the horizontal line that faces you.
    2. Back and forth along the vertical line that faces you.
    3. A rotating clockwise motion around the circle.
    4. A rotating counterclockwise motion around the circle.

- "Warm up" first by voluntarily moving the pendulum a few times in all of the four possible directions.

- Your subconscious should then be asked to signify which motion is one of the four answers to your questions. To determine this, hold the pendulum motionless over the circle where the two lines cross and ask your subconscious to do the following:

    - Move the pendulum in the direction that will be a "Yes" answer.
    - Move the pendulum in the direction that will be a "No" answer.
    - Move the pendulum in the direction that will be an "I Don't Know" answer.
    - Move the pendulum in the direction that will signify "I Don't Wish to Answer."

- Give your subconscious a few seconds to do this, making sure that you're not consciously forcing a movement. Your subconscious will move it.

- After you have established which movement determines which of the four answers you may receive, you are then ready to use the pendulum to ask your subconscious questions such as:

    > **"Have you, my subconscious mind, fully accepted my suggestion to make healthier meal choices?"**

    > **"Has my suggestion to be completely open and receptive to intuitive guidance taken firm hold in my subconscious mind?"**

- If you want to test the acceptance of a suggestion *immediately* following self-hypnosis, you can ask questions such as:

> "Have you, my subconscious mind, fully accepted the suggestion I gave myself during the self-hypnosis session just concluded?"

> "Will my conscious thinking now be subconsciously influenced by the suggestion I gave myself during the self-hypnosis session just concluded?"

- Only a very slight movement is necessary to get an answer, providing that it continues for a while in the same direction.

- By keeping your eyes fixed on the pendulum during questioning, the pendulum will produce better results.

CHEVREUL PENDULUM TESTING CIRCLE

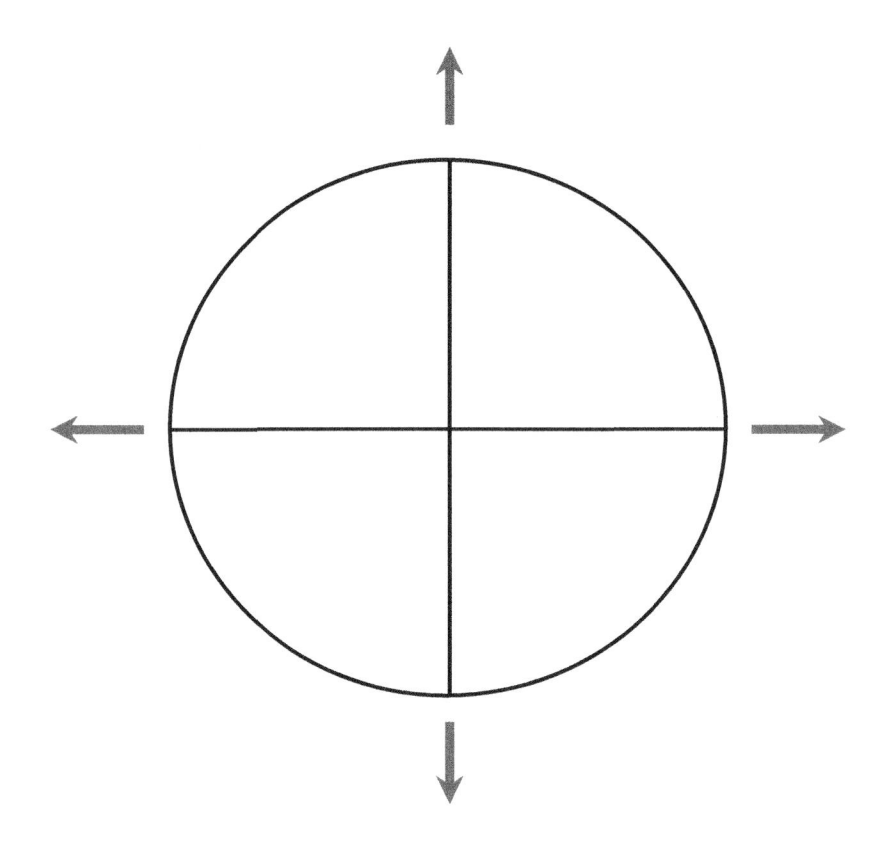

Fill in below after your subconscious has responded to which motion means which of the four possible answers.

"Yes" is a _____ motion.

"No" is a _____ motion.

"I Don't Know" is a _____ motion.

"I Don't Wish to Answer" is a _____ motion.

IDEOMOTOR FINGER TEST

This test is based on the same idea as the Chevreul Pendulum Test. However, instead of using a pendulum to get answers from your subconscious mind, you use the fingers of your writing hand.

You may find this test a little harder to master than using a pendulum, but it has an advantage over the pendulum method, since it can be used when you are in the presence of others—at work, for example—without anyone detecting that you are engaged in anything out of the ordinary.

PROCEDURE

- Place your writing hand on the arm of a chair or in your lap, palm down.

- Stretch out your fingers easily so that they have the freedom to move.

- Ask your subconscious to move any of your fingers upward to signify any of the four possible answers you pose to your subconscious mind: "Yes," "No," "I don't know," or "I don't wish to answer."

- Look directly at your fingers as you ask which finger will mean which answer.

- Movements of the fingers in this test are usually slight, though not always so. You may first notice a tingling sensation in the finger that is about to lift up. That finger may also shake or tremble slightly as it lifts.

- The finger should finally lift up to a pointing position. As in the pendulum method, make no voluntary effort to help the movement along.

- Once you have determined which finger means which answer, proceed to ask questions of your subconscious mind as you do with the pendulum method.

NOTE:

When first learning this technique, the finger movements may seem slow or slight to respond. However, if you use this technique often, your fingers will begin to respond more quickly. This technique can even be used when standing and talking to someone, getting responses from your fingers as your hand rests lightly on the side of your thigh. It is a technique well worth any time you spend on perfecting and mastering it.

TESTING A SUGGESTION DURING HYPNOSIS

There is no better time to find out if a self-improvement suggestion has taken root in your subconscious mind than *during* hypnosis, when you are *already* in close contact with your subconscious. The best way to conduct this test is through Ideomotor Finger responses. Here is the technique:

- While in a state of hypnosis, give yourself a self-improvement suggestion, repeating that suggestion slowly and deliberately a number of times.

- Then ask yourself questions that are phrased so you can get a simple "Yes" or "No" answer, such as:

    > **"Have you, my subconscious mind, fully accepted my preceding suggestion?"**

    > **"Will you, my subconscious mind, now gear my thinking to act out my preceding suggestion in my daily living?"**

    - If you fail to get either a "Yes" or "No" answer, it could mean that your suggestion was not phrased clearly to your subconscious. Rephrase your suggestion and try again.

    - If you get a "No" answer, do not give up with just one sitting. Keep repeating the same suggestion to yourself for a few days while in hypnosis.

- Double-check the test. If you still receive a "No" answer as to whether your subconscious mind has fully accepted your suggestion, ask yourself the following:

    > **"Is the suggestion *beginning* to take hold in my subconscious mind?"**

    > **"Has this suggestion taken *more* hold today than it did yesterday?"**

- If you get a "Yes" answer, then keep at it day after day, until the suggestion has been *fully* accepted.

- If you continue to get a "No" answer, and you can't find the reason for the resistance on your own through self-analysis, you may need the assistance of a professional psychologist or therapist to probe for the resistance factor and remove it.

VISUALIZATION

Although programming the subconscious mind with affirmations during meditation or suggestions during self-hypnosis is a powerful way to improve your life, those affirmations and suggestions can be even more effective when reinforced through visualization.

Visualization is not just about *seeing* something in your mind, it is about *feeling* it as a reality in your life—as something that has already been obtained or is in the process of being materialized in physical reality. For example:

- **DURING MEDITATION**: If your affirmation is about doing something you have been avoiding doing, visualize yourself having just completed it, and allow a feeling of accomplishment to come over you.

- **DURING SELF-HYPNOSIS**: If your suggestion is about getting along with someone who constantly irritates you, see and feel yourself talking to that person in a calm, easy manner, maintaining your poise no matter what he or she says.

While it is not absolutely necessary to use visualization to supplement your affirmations or suggestions, it has been found that the mind tends to follow through on visual imagery, especially if the same image is constantly repeated over time during your self-hypnosis or meditation sessions.

What follows are two techniques that utilize visualization for manifesting your desires, and one for seeking answers from your Higher Mind.

CREATIVE LIGHT TECHNIQUE

This visualization technique is based on the idea that all things manifested in this universe come forth from the Creative Light of Universal Intelligence, or God.

- First, place yourself in a state of meditation or self-hypnosis.

- Become relaxed and sensitive to the Presence of Infinite Mind as a Creative Light at the center of your mind.

- Imagine and visualize that whatever you desire is being materialized in the glow of this Light. See, think, and feel this as a reality.

- As you do this, silently repeat the following affirmation to yourself:

    "What I visualize is already mine through the power of the Creative Light-Presence of the Perfect Universal Mind of God."

Remember that visualizations are always more effective when repeated on a daily basis.

DAILY THOUGHT TECHNIQUE

This technique is designed to reinforce whatever you visualize during your formal, daily meditation practice or self-hypnosis session.

The basis for this technique is the fact that during the course of your daily activities, your most-wanted desires will periodically surface to your conscious mind as thoughts. Instead of letting those desires remain only as thoughts—thoughts that will once again recede back into your unconscious—you proceed in the following manner:

- When the thought of a desire enters your conscious mind, immediately visualize it as already a reality in your life.

- Mentally picture yourself as already having your desire, and feel the exhilaration of the emotion of already possessing it.

This technique alone is so powerful in its psychic effect, I have come to believe it to be more powerful at times than many formal procedures. Use it daily and you will be amazed at the results it produces in materializing your desires.

IMPORTANT NOTE:

It is important to keep in mind that life-improving ideas actually originate in the Consciousness of God within you. However, your ego can often take a divine idea and turn it into something it was never meant to be. No matter what you are visualizing for yourself, your job is to seek alignment with God's Will for you, and be open and receptive to the manifestation of whatever is best for your soul's purpose in this lifetime.

Remember, too, that there is sufficient abundance in this universe for all, so visualize only that which will not take away from another person. And if someone else plays a part in what you are visualizing, do not try to force your will on him or her. What is right for you will happen in time—God's time.

INNER SKY TECHNIQUE

Visualization can not only be used to help you manifest your desires, it can also help you receive answers to questions via your Higher Mind.

As you know, when you meditate you open a channel from the surface level of your mind to the deeper, Universal part of your mind. Through that channel, intuitive direction from your Higher Mind can reach your surface consciousness.

This generally happens in the form of hunches or inspirations that spontaneously arise while meditating. However, there may be times when you want immediate and direct answers to certain questions confronting you in your life. When that is the case, use the following technique:

- Place yourself in a state of meditation or self-hypnosis and become as relaxed as possible.

- Imagine that as you look into the interior region of your forehead, you are, in fact, looking into an Infinite Sky of Inner Consciousness.

- See this sky as dark, infinite space before you.

- Into it, ask and direct your question or questions.

- Ask that the answers to your questions come from Infinite Mind and be written across your Infinite Sky of Inner Consciousness in white letters.

- Practice starting slowly, asking your name, address, and so on, before getting to more meaningful questions for which you seek answers and direction.

INNER VISION EXPANSION

Here is a technique you can use to increase the visual area of your Third Eye, expanding it from the interior of your forehead to the entire area inside your head:

1. If you are in a sitting position, imagine that on the wall directly in front of you there is a circle about three feet in diameter. If you are in a reclining position, imagine this circle is on the ceiling directly above you.

2. With your eyes closed, let your eyes travel clockwise around the circle seven times.

3. Then reverse the direction and go counterclockwise seven times.

4. Do this very slowly, moving your eyes under your eyelids.

5. At this point the inside of your head will begin to have a radiance around the line that your eyes traveled.

6. Within that circle of radiance your inner vision will lighten, allowing you to see more clearly and expansively.

A METAPHYSICAL WAY OF LIFE

LIVING METAPHYSICALLY

The word "metaphysics" originates from a combination of two Greek words—"meta" and "physika"—meaning "beyond physics." In most dictionaries, metaphysics is defined as a branch of philosophy that deals with the underlying nature of reality.

In today's world, metaphysics has become a general label encompassing many fields of interest. Those fields include, but are not limited to: parapsychology, mysticism, yoga, dream analysis, astrology, transcendentalism, reincarnation, and more.

I believe, however, that the foremost goal of anyone interested in metaphysics should be the firsthand experience of God's Presence—the Ultimate Source of All. That is why my focus is on connecting through meditation to the Consciousness of God that resides in the innermost center of the mind. Through that contact with Universal Intelligence, one becomes God-guided in life, which improves every single facet of daily living. When viewed from that perspective, metaphysics is not just some kind of esoteric exercise; it is a very practical pursuit.

Obviously, then, when it comes to living a metaphysical life, the most important aspect is practicing Mystical Meditation daily. Improving your life through affirmations and self-hypnotic suggestions also plays a significant role. However, there is still more to living life metaphysically than meditation and self-programming.

Also involved is closely monitoring the thoughts you think and carefully choosing the words you speak, because both have unseen power. How you respond to cycles in your life also plays a part, for even when you practice a metaphysical way of life, you will still experience both high and low periods over time.

In this final section of *Meditation Dynamics*, I will show you how to take charge of your life metaphysically, resulting in a life that is more positive, fulfilling, productive, and aware.

CONTROLLING YOUR THOUGHTS

Thoughts have power. A metaphysical way of life includes taking charge of your thoughts by carefully monitoring and controlling them. Here are the basic principles and practices involved:

PRINCIPLES

- Every thought you think has a psychic energy.

- Every thought you think enters your subconscious mind, and through the subconscious mind, enters the psychic realm.

- Every thought you think is important, for every thought attracts its like nature to you on a psychic level.

- Every thought you think that is positive in nature attracts positive results to you psychically.

- Every thought you think that is negative in nature attracts negative results to you psychically.

- Every thought you think has a magnetic property to it in the psychic realm of mind.

- Every thought you think that is loving, therefore, attracts love.

- Every thought you think that is prosperous, therefore, attracts prosperity.

- Every thought you think fills the psychic atmosphere of where you work or live; therefore, think positive, good thoughts.

- Every thought you think starts out psychically, but then returns to you in physical manifestation, whether it be as a person, thing, condition, or circumstance; therefore, as you choose your thoughts, you choose your life.

- Every thought you think affects your health and happiness.

- Every thought you think has creative psychic power for good or for ill.

- Every thought you think will make you a master or slave of life.

PRACTICES

- Become aware that you are thinking.

- Be aware of every thought that you are thinking.

- Learn to divide your mind into two parts—that which is thinking, and a Master Control Awareness of what you are thinking. Through the Master Control Awareness, censor or accept every thought.

REGARDING NEGATIVE THOUGHTS

- The moment you think a negative or destructive thought, tell yourself: "I nullify that thought so that it does not enter my subconscious mind."

- Every time you find yourself thinking a negative or depressing thought, see how fast you can get rid of it through the above affirmation.

- Every time you think an unkind thought toward someone, catch yourself and say: "Guide me to understand why they are the way they are, so through that understanding I can bless them."

- If you find it difficult to bless someone due to a great deal of ill-feeling, say the following: "I call upon the Presence of God within me to forgive the person whom I, at the moment, do not seem to have the power to forgive."

- Remember that there is a positive and negative side to every person and thing. If you start to think about the negative, catch yourself and then immediately begin to think about the positive side.

- Work constantly on trying to shorten the time it takes to censor or reject a negative thought.

- Constantly be aware of the fact that your every thought has the psychic power to either clear up your problems or keep them alive and attract even more to you.

REGARDING POSITIVE THOUGHTS

The moment a positive thought about yourself, your life, your abilities, or your possibilities enters your mind, make it a greater reality in your mind by doing the following:

- Rather than just letting the positive thought pass through your conscious mind and then enter your subconscious, enforce the power of the thought by adding these powerful words to it: "AND SO IT IS!"

- Repeat those words more than once for even greater acceptance of your positive thought by your mind.

- As you say those words, feel that your positive thought has been given added energy as it travels into the psychic atmosphere, attracting its corresponding good to you.

- Do this every day, with every positive thought you think, and more and more you will see the influence it is having on your positive mental attitude, and in the further increase of good in your life.

- Do not underestimate the power of this simple method over your life and mind.

CONTROLLING YOUR WORDS

Just as your thoughts have power, the words you speak have power, too—a lot of power. This is because the energy of spoken words is the magnified energy of your thoughts. Therefore, a metaphysical way of life also includes taking charge of your words by carefully choosing them. Here are the basic principles and practices involved:

PRINCIPLES

- Every word you speak is a vibration of psychic energy coming forth from your mouth.

- Every word you speak fills the immediate atmosphere with an unseen, but very real psychic vibrational energy.

- Every word you speak affects, on a psychic vibrational level, the physical atmosphere in which it is spoken.

- Every word you speak either cleanses or poisons the psychic atmosphere in which it is spoken.

- Every word you speak sets up a psychic vibrational power in direct proportion to the intensity of force or volume with which it is spoken.

- Every word you speak affects human beings, animals, plants, and inanimate objects on a psychic vibrational level.

- Every word you speak is like an invocation to the universe to attract to you the likeness of your words.

- Every word you speak is a creative vibration of psychic energy that draws to itself that which is of a like nature—positive or negative.

- Every word you speak that is positive creates a healing, harmonious, youthful, and beautifying vibrational energy throughout your body.

- Every word you speak that is negative creates a self-destructive, not youthful, beauty-destroying vibration throughout your body.

PRACTICES

- Always be aware of what you are saying, and how you are saying it.

- Always be aware of the words you are choosing to say.

- Always be aware that every word leaving your mouth is a vibration of psychic energy.

REGARDING NEGATIVE WORDS

- Avoid the use of negative words. They set up and attract negative vibrational reactions.

- When thinking or speaking about conditions or others, avoid negative curse terms. Their mental or verbal utilization can only attract to you increased negativity from people or conditions.

- If you have the feeling to curse someone or something, catch yourself, mentally pause for a moment, and bless the person or condition instead. This will not only attract positive psychic vibrations to you, but it will also help clear up the situation.

- If you have something unpleasant that has to be spoken of, mentally pause for a moment and try to use words that will take the psychic sting out of what you have to say.

- If a negative or destructive word slips out, think to yourself or say out loud, "I nullify the word(s) I have just used," and bless that person or condition instead.

REGARDING POSITIVE WORDS

- Cultivate the use of positive words, for they set up and attract other positive vibrational reactions.

- Carefully guard the volume and pitch of your voice when speaking. Try to develop and maintain a tone of voice that is harmonious.

- Smile when you speak, or at least have a pleasant facial expression, and you can increase the positive vibrational energies of your spoken words.

- Learn and practice to mentally pause for a moment before speaking, trying to frame your thoughts into positive words.

- Be silent about your desires and goals. Keeping silent builds psychic energy in your mind, thus giving more magnetism to your psychic thought currents as they travel into the creative psychic medium of Universal Mind.

- Do not speak needlessly and talk just for the sake of talking. This way you build up a psychic energy reserve for the vibrational force or power of your spoken words.

CONTROLLING CYCLES IN YOUR LIFE

As I pointed out in the introduction to this section of the book, even when you are living metaphysically, over time you will still experience both high and low periods in your life. Just as there is spring, summer, fall, and winter in the cycles of nature, there are similar cycles taking place within the affairs of humanity, and even within your own mind:

- Like spring, there is a period when changes are given birth within your mind.

- Like summer, there is a period for you to assimilate those changes and grow.

- Like fall, there is a period when growth stops—a time for introspection on what has changed.

- Like winter, there is a period of seeming dormancy—a time for considering what changes the beginning of the next cycle may bring.

Understanding this cyclical pattern is important, because your inner state of mind ultimately affects what is manifested in your outer life. If you practice metaphysical principles you have more control over these cycles and their progression than the average person does, which positively affects your life experience and enhances your upward personal growth.

What follows are four graphs—with accompanying explanations—that illustrate the result of various responses to life's ups and downs:

CYCLES OF THE AVERAGE PERSON

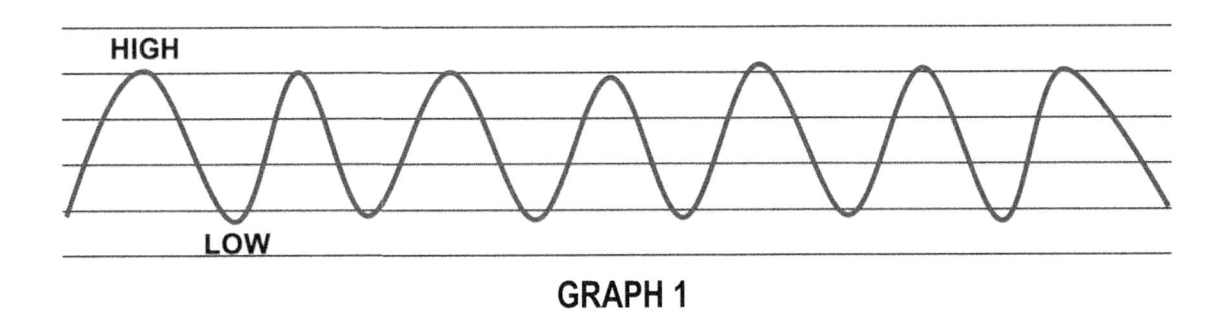

GRAPH 1

Graph 1 illustrates the experience of the average person who has little or no understanding of cycles, and is therefore in the grips of a collective psychic energy that binds this person to the highs and lows of society around him.

- This individual does little or nothing within the mind to control the peaks and valleys in his or her life, leaving those highs and lows to the collective chance of society.

- If collective society is prospering, this person prospers; if not, this person struggles.

- The high periods generally come only so often, and the low periods with greater frequency.

- Therefore, the highs seem higher, and the lows lower.

CYCLES OF A NEGATIVE PERSON

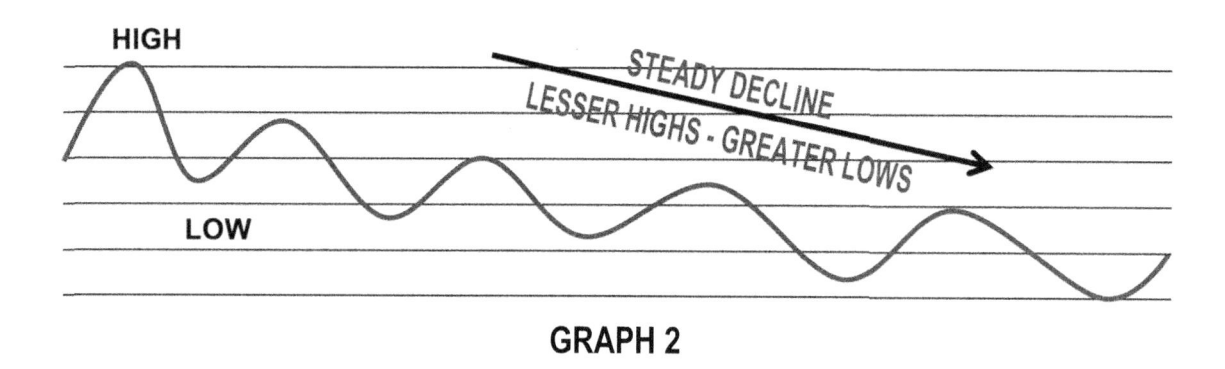

HIGH

STEADY DECLINE
LESSER HIGHS - GREATER LOWS

LOW

GRAPH 2

Graph 2 illustrates how a negative person experiences cycles. Driven by previous traumatic failure patterns, this person consciously or unconsciously gears his or her mind for decline.

- The mind of this individual vibrates to the energy of chronic failure.

- He or she considers the highs as not really all that good, but rather as merely a breather before the inevitable coming of the next low period of failure and frustration.

- As a result, this person experiences life's cycles as perpetually declining.

- Each high is not as high as the one before, and each low is lower than the one before.

BALANCED CYCLES
OF A PERSON PRACTICING METAPHYSICS

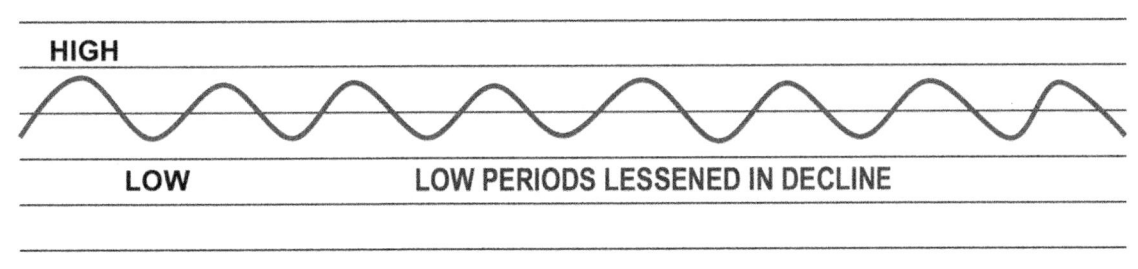

HIGH

LOW   LOW PERIODS LESSENED IN DECLINE

GRAPH 3

Graph 3 illustrates what I call the "Balanced Cycles" experienced by a person who is putting metaphysical principles into practice. By maintaining a positive attitude about life and himself or herself, practicing Mystical Meditation, and conducting positive-thought self-programming, this individual begins to balance the high and low periods in his or her life.

- Balanced Cycles are usually experienced during the first six months of daily metaphysical practice.

- For the first time, a balancing of polarities in the mental energies of this person's mind is being achieved. Thus, a steadfastness of mind emerges.

- The life flow of this person adjusts itself to a psychic equilibrium.

- When the low part of a cycle comes, it is not much of a psychic dip.

- Similarly, when the high part of a cycle arrives, it is not an overreaction.

PROGRESSIVE CYCLES
OF A PERSON PRACTICING METAPHYSICS

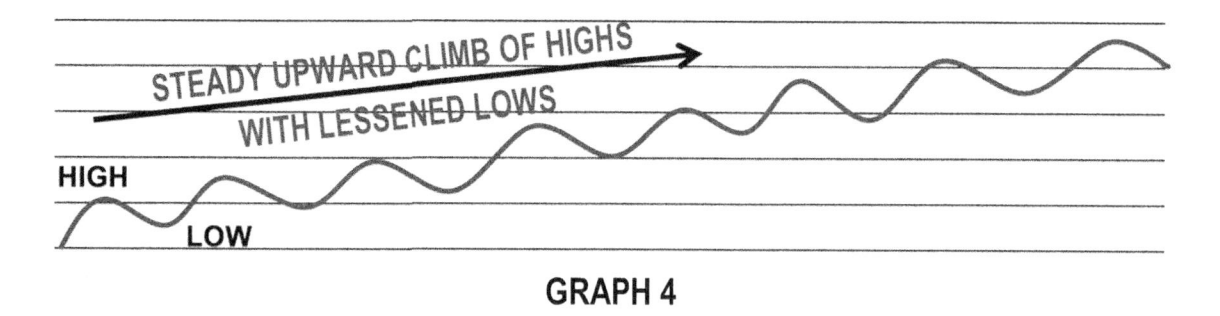

STEADY UPWARD CLIMB OF HIGHS WITH LESSENED LOWS

HIGH
LOW

GRAPH 4

Graph 4 illustrates what I call the "Progressive Cycles" experienced by a person who—over time—has consistently maintained a steadfast or balanced mind through daily metaphysical practices.

- This person experiences a steady, upward climb in life.

- Each high is higher than the previous one, and each low ceases to be as low as the one before.

- Even during the low part of a cycle, this individual does not fall that far down.

- This person will experience Progressive Cycles for life, as long as he or she continues to put metaphysical principles into practice on a daily basis.

GUIDELINES FOR ACHIEIVING BALANCED OR PROGRESSIVE CYCLES

WHEN YOU ARE IN THE LOW PART OF A CYCLE

Monitor your thinking and nullify all negative thoughts. Instead, use that time to program your mind with positive thoughts.

- This will build a positive psychic energy reservoir in your subconscious, so when you move into the high part of a cycle, it will rise higher than before.

- Similarly, when you move into the low part of a cycle, it will not dip as low as before, because there will be no place in your subconscious thought patterns for it.

Do not take a low period as a reversal in your life. Think of it as what it is—a chance to assimilate the results of your previous high period, and a time to prepare your mind for the next high period. A good affirmation for that is:

"I am assimilating the results of my previous high period, and I am preparing my mind for new growth in my next high period through the Presence of the God-Power of my being."

WHEN YOU ARE IN THE HIGH PART OF A CYCLE

Don't relax your spiritual practices, feeling that you only need them when you are down. On the contrary—continue to program your mind with positive thoughts and meditate more often. That way you can obtain the very highest accomplishments during the high part of the cycle you are in. Consider always that the God-Power of your being is intuitively guiding you in ever-upward growth via the cycles of your life, and affirm the following:

"My mind is under the direction of the limitless God-Mind-Power within me to reach the zenith of my present high period."

ATTUNING THROUGH YOUR DAILY ACTIVITIES

Although the most powerful way to attune yourself to the God-Power within you is by programming your subconscious mind with affirmations during meditation, you can also attune yourself by consciously using affirmations in conjunction with your daily activities. Doing so makes your daily tasks and responsibilities easier and helps you obtain positive results more readily.

What follows are some suggested affirmations to hold in your mind as you engage in your daily activities. It is not necessary for you to use the exact words as they appear here. It is far more important for you to maintain the general idea in your consciousness.

WAKING

"I dedicate this day to God within me, the True Self of my being. It is the Power of God working through me that lives in me this day."

BATHING

"The psychic cleansing power in the water I use washes away negative vibrations, and I am left in a clean, positive vibration."

GETTING DRESSED

"I project spiritually cleansing psychic light into my clothes, and my clothes are filled with positive vibrational energies."

COOKING

"The heat that I use to cook with is like a psychic-spiritual fire that cleanses all negative vibrations from the food that I am preparing, and it leaves only positive energy vibrations for the well-being of my body."

EATING
"I send forth the thought of blessing into the food that I am about to eat, and the aura of my thought surrounds it with positive vibrations. When I eat this blessed food, therefore, it will produce further positive vibrations of health in the energies of my body."

PAYING
"Whatever money now leaves my hand will return to me many times over through my awareness of the Law of Divine Circulation."

BANKING
"God is my supply, and my account is supplied to meet my every need."

GROCERY SHOPPING
"I bless this place as a physical channel for the nourishment of my body, and I bless my pocketbook as God-Power fills it so I may purchase what I need."

GENERAL SHOPPING
"I am led by the God-Power within me to the right store, for the right item, at the right price."

CLEANING THE HOUSE
"As I clean the house, I am aware that I am being moved by the Divine Power within me—erasing the negative and putting the positive in its place."

DRIVING
"I bless my car as a vehicle through which I may gain greater experience, thus furthering wisdom, and through wisdom, happiness."

WITH MEDIA (Internet, Newspapers, Television, Radio)
"I am aware and Divinely protected from the lack of evolution of this planet, and my consciousness vibrates only to that which adds to my happiness, awareness, well-being, and prosperity."

BEING COURTEOUS
"My mind is aware of any opportunity to be courteous to someone, knowing that I put into motion a chain reaction that helps others grow spiritually."

BEING FRIENDLY
"I express warmth towards my friends, and, above all, an understanding of the underlying factors in their lives."

BEING AFFECTIONATE
"I am open in my expression of affection to those who are dear to me, but I do not try to bind them or imprison them to me through the use of affectionate expression."

BEING ENCOURAGING
"Whenever I am with someone, I am alert to their assets and encourage them through a sincere compliment."

RETIRING
"To God within me, I dedicate the efforts of this day, my soul, and my existence. I thank You for having lived in Your Presence one more day, and for bestowing upon those near and dear to me Your love and blessings, peace of mind and body, health of mind and body, and your Spiritual Presence.

DAILY FORMAT FOR LIVING METAPHYSICALLY

This book has covered Mystical Meditation, self-programming through Affirmative Meditation and Suggestive Self-Hypnosis, the power of Visualization, the importance of Controlling Your Thoughts and Words, and much more. You now have the tools you need to live life metaphysically—to enjoy a life of lasting happiness, fulfillment, peace, inspiration, success, and love.

However, metaphysics is not something you only turn to when life has gotten tough. To reap the rewards of a metaphysical way of life, you must put metaphysical principles into practice daily. Daily! So, to conclude this book, here is the format I recommend that you follow each and every day:

MYSTICAL MEDITATION: Using the techniques you have learned in this book, practice Mystical Meditation at least once daily. If you can regulate your schedule, it would be even more advantageous to practice twice daily—once in the morning and once in the evening.

AFFIRMATIVE MEDITATION: At least once daily, program your subconscious mind with affirmations from this book, or others you have created according to the suggested guidelines.

CREATIVE LIGHT VISUALIZATION: After you have practiced Affirmative Meditation, practice Creative Light Visualization once daily.

DAILY THOUGHT VISUALIZATION: Every time the thought of a desire enters your mind, through mental pictures immediately visualize yourself as already possessing it.

CONTROLLING YOUR THOUGHTS: Constantly monitor your thinking as you engage in your daily activities. Nullify negative thoughts before they enter your subconscious mind, and maintain a positive attitude about everything.

CONTROLLING YOUR WORDS: Constantly be aware of what you are saying and how you are saying it. Avoid negative conversation and foul language. Speak positively and with conviction.

INSTANTANEOUS MEDITATION: Whenever you need relaxation or regeneration, set aside time to practice instantaneous meditation.

SLEEP PROGRAMMING: Every night before falling asleep, feed your mind positive thoughts, which will become deeply seated in your subconscious during sleep and align that part of your mind with your Higher Mind.

ABOUT THE AUTHOR

As far back as he could remember, Dr. Paul Leon Masters was drawn to the mysteries of life, the universe, the human mind and soul, and the presence of a higher intelligence behind creation.

In 1959 Dr. Masters established the Institute of Parapsychology in Beverly Hills, California, to research and explore higher states of consciousness by utilizing advanced forms of meditation and self-hypnotic techniques. During the course of those studies and explorations Dr. Masters achieved what is generally considered to be the ultimate goal of meditation—mystical union with Universal Consciousness, or the Mind of God.

In 1965 Dr. Masters founded the National Metaphysics Institute for the study of metaphysics and the ordination of metaphysical ministers. Since meditation has always been an integral part in his life and teachings, Dr. Masters required all students of the Institute to study and practice meditation, and in 1973 he introduced into his teachings a formal course of study called "Meditation Dynamics," which is the foundation for this book.

In 1976 Dr. Masters replaced the National Metaphysics Institute with the University of Metaphysics, granting students of the University non-secular bachelor's, master's, and doctoral degrees, as well as ministerial ordinations. During this time, Dr. Masters presented numerous public presentations to packed auditoriums in the Los Angeles area, and he began offering his programs throughout the United States via distance-learning. Soon, Dr. Masters' programs became known internationally, and in 1989 he founded the International Metaphysical Ministry to accommodate the enormous worldwide interest in his teachings.

Between 2002 and 2004, Dr. Masters moved his base of operations to Sedona, Arizona, a place well-known for its heightened spiritual energy. There, he founded the University of Sedona to operate in concert with the University of Metaphysics. As divisions of the International Metaphysical Ministry, both universities have a curriculum that is strictly non-secular and theological in nature, and they have become the world's largest schools of their kind, with students and graduates in 120 countries.

After Dr. Masters' passing in 2016, all three organizations continue to operate in Sedona with a dedicated staff working under the direction of a board of trustees.

Dr. Masters' contributions to the field of mystical psychology were those of a trailblazer, and he rightly deserves recognition for being one of the world's foremost teachers of metaphysical doctors, teachers, and ministers. The education he provided over the years has produced an international alumni and student population that reaches out to transform the world. The evolving curriculum, based on decades of higher consciousness research, offers timeless teachings that connect people to their higher self—their soul—and the Presence of God within.

For more information about Dr. Masters, his lifetime of work, and his legacy, please visit www.universityofmetaphysics.com/history.

ADVANCED METAPHYSICAL STUDIES

Not only is meditation the most important aspect of living a metaphysical life, but it is also the very foundation of almost all metaphysical teachings. Most metaphysical concepts and their resulting philosophies of living have been arrived at through knowledge gained in meditation. Even wisdom regarding the ultimate nature of reality—of life after death, astral dimensions, and so on—has likewise been gleaned from meditational experiences.

As it is with meditation itself, studying metaphysics and applying its principles can benefit your life in many ways. Among those benefits is the fact that a formal education in metaphysics can be used to support a metaphysical career—a career as a life coach, pastoral counselor, metaphysical author, speaker, teacher, or spiritual healer . . . just to name a few.

With a degree from The University of Metaphysics or The University of Sedona—both founded by Dr. Masters—you can earn the credentials that will enable you to use your gifts and knowledge to help others as a professional metaphysical practitioner. Those credentials include:

- Bachelor of Metaphysical Science, B.Msc.
- Ordained Metaphysical Minister Certificate
- Metaphysical Practitioner Diploma
- Master of Metaphysical Science, M.Msc.
- Doctor of Philosophy, Ph.D., specializing in various fields.
- Doctor of Divinity, D.D., specializing in a variety of fields.
- Doctor of Ministry, D.Min., specializing in an array of fields.
- And many more Doctoral degrees are available.

All of our courses are distance learning, which means you can study from the comfort of your own home and on your own schedule. Should the need arise, our faculty and staff are available to personally advise you in regard to our curriculum. Plus, thanks to generous donations from our alumni, we are able to provide affordable tuition through scholarships. Just be sure to "Enroll with Scholarship" when you visit either of our websites.

For more information, visit us at www.universityofmetaphysics.com
or www.universityofsedona.com.

Email us at uom@metaphysics.com.

Or call us in the United States at 1-888-866-4685
or internationally at 1-928-203-0730.

MORE SPIRITUAL RESOURCES

BOOKS

Mystical Insights: Knowing the Unknown

Dr. Masters' soul's fulfillment was to share how Universal Presence and psychic/mystical energy factors influence every aspect of our lives. Dr. Masters explores these important concepts and shares his wisdom in this enlightening book, available in both Paperback, eBook, and AudioBook editions. For more information and/or to order your copy, go to "Dr. Masters' Books" under the "Store" heading at metaphysics.com. Or, contact the University of Metaphysics directly at uom@metaphysics.com.

Spiritual Mind Power Affirmations

During his Sunday services, Dr. Paul Leon Masters presented a large number of inspirational lectures. Almost all of them began with a meditation or healing treatment, after which he presented a teaching that included a set of affirmation statements. This book is a collection of the affirmations Dr. Masters presented in 100 of his lectures. For more information and/or to order your copy—available in both Paperback and eBook editions—go to "Dr. Masters' Books" under the "Store" heading at metaphysics.com. Or, contact the University of Metaphysics directly at uom@metaphysics.com.

AUDIO RECORDINGS

Daily "Improve Your Life" Audio Messages

Dr. Masters' daily audio messages and meditations can help you successfully navigate daily life and inspire you to rise above any challenges you may have. To listen to these inspiring messages, go to universityofmetaphysics.com, where we post them daily on the "Daily 'Improve Your Life' Messages" page listed under "Free Sources."

Weekly Mystical Insights

In addition to the fifty mystical insights Dr. Masters shared in his book, *Mystical Insights: Knowing the Unknown*, we publish more of Dr. Masters' mystical insights each week at universityofmetaphysics.com. Just go to the "Mystical Insights" page listed under "Free Resources," where you will find both written and recorded versions.

Timeless Wisdom Series

For more than fifty years Dr. Masters researched higher consciousness, synthesizing the results of that research with science, psychology, and the mystical teachings of Christ and others. We are now releasing audio recordings of hundreds of his lectures that haven't been available since they were first recorded. You will find these enlightening lectures at metaphysics.com/timeless-wisdom.

The Voice of Meditation

Dr. Masters has been considered by many to be foremost in guiding people into and through meditation. On our Voice of Meditation website, you will find 31 audio recordings of his higher consciousness meditations, which people all around the world have been benefitting from for decades. Just go to voiceofmeditation.com.

VIDEO RECORDINGS

Inspirational Lectures

Every lecture that formed the basis for Dr. Masters' book, *Spiritual Mind Power Affirmations*, is available to you as a Video Download or DVD, as well as an Audio Download or CD. Just go to metaphysics.com/all-lectures to find all 100 of these lectures—and more. Or, you can go to universityofmetaphysics.com, where we feature a different video lecture every week on the "Weekly Inspirational Lectures" page listed under "Free Resources."

NEWSLETTER

Weekly Newsletter

Delivered by email every Sunday, this free weekly newsletter offers a variety of informative and inspiring material. In addition to a link to one of Dr. Masters' Inspirational Lectures, it includes links to one of his Mystical Insights, his Daily Audio Message, and more. We encourage you to sign up for this wonderful and convenient spiritual resource. Go to universityofmetaphysics.com/newsletter.

For further information, please call:
In USA: 1-888-866-4685
International: 1-928-203-0730
or email uom@metaphysics.com

www.internationalmetaphysicalministry.com
www.universityofmetaphysics.com
www.universityofsedona.com
www.metaphysics.com
www.theocentricpsychology.com
www.voiceofmeditation.com

Printed in Great Britain
by Amazon